# HOW TO GET FROM THE

# AIRPORT
# TO THE
# CITY

## ALL AROUND THE
## WORLD

# HOW TO GET FROM THE

# AIRPORT
## TO THE
## CITY

## ALL AROUND THE
## WORLD

## NORMAN CRAMPTON

M. Evans and Company    New York

Library of Congress Cataloging-in-Publication Data

Crampton, Norman.
  How to get from the airport to the city all around the world.

  1. Access to airports.    I. Title.
HE9797.4.A2C72    1988      387.7'362      87-37975.


ISBN 0-87131-583-1

M. Evans and Company, Inc.
216 East 49 Street
New York, New York 10017

Manufactured in the United States of America

9 8 7 6 5 4 3 2 1

# INTRODUCTION

In the air, others worry about getting you safely from point A to point B. But on the ground you're on your own. And unless you're returning home or being met by a welcoming committee, getting from the airport to point C may require information you don't have. That's what this book is for.

At most airports there is more than one way to get to your final destination—taxi, airport shuttle, public bus, metro, helicopter, water taxi, rental car. The right choice will make the best match with your schedule and budget. This *Cheap/Smart Guide* will help you make the right choice by providing the data you need for an informed decision: departure and running times, costs, frequencies, routes, and all the other details of airport ground transportation.

## Symbols & Assumptions

This eighth annual edition of *How To Get From the Airport to the City All Around the World* contains data for 376 airports, arranged alphabetically by the name of the principal nearby city. The information is presented in the same sequence at each entry, beginning with the name of the airport and the distance and direction from the city.

Symbols—the same ones you will see in many airports—are used to identify the transportation options. Following is a key to the symbols including an explanation of the kinds of information presented at each, as well as certain assumptions that apply throughout.

🚕 **Taxicab** The first fare quoted is the cost to city center of the principal nearby city, in local currency with U.S. translation. Then: extra charges, if any; and tipping custom if there might be some question about what to give the driver. Assumptions: cab is metered; large enough for four, possibly five passengers with baggage; and one fare covers all. Exceptions are noted.

🚐 **Airport Coach, Shuttle, Limo, Van** Details: name of service, operating hours and schedule, route, fare, conveniences. Assume that this service, like the others, departs from or adjacent to baggage claim. Driver usually hoists baggage on and off as part of routine service. Hotels and transportation centers are the principal stops.

🚌 **Public Bus** Number, name, schedule, travel time, fare, baggage space if any. These buses usually make many stops on their way into the city; they seldom serve hotels. But in selected cities—London and Rome, for example—riding the public bus from the airport provides a close-up look at city life that might pass by too quickly in a cab, for example.

🚊 **Metro, Subway, Tram, Train** Destination, frequency, operating hours, travel time, fare, baggage space, comparative comfort. Numerous European cities have laid rail to the airport and shown what a good means of transportation this can be. Brussels, Geneva, London-Heathrow, Amsterdam, Frankfurt, and Barcelona are just a few examples. The United States has fewer airport rail links but some very good services. In Chicago, Cleveland, Philadelphia, and Atlanta, the rail station is within the airport. In Boston, Oakland, Washington, D.C., and New York-JFK, a good rail connection is just a short shuttle ride away.

🚁 **Helicopter** Schedule, fare. Such air taxis tend to come and go. This edition lists service at Boston, New York-JFK, and Los Angeles.

🚗 **Rental Cars** Companies with counters in the terminal as well as others serving the airport are listed, alphabetically.

**P** **Parking** Daily short-term (ST) and long-term (LT) rates are given in local and U.S. currency. Assume there is a free shuttle bus from baggage claim to the more distant, long-term lot.

## Free Transport

One very common means of airport ground transportation is not listed here. It is the free shuttle service provided by many hotels and motels. So if you're headed for a hostelry, check the bank of "Courtesy" telephones in baggage claim.

## Accuracy

We have taken care to present accurate information. But remember that services, schedules, travel times, fares, and foreign exchange rates change from time to time. If certain data are critical to your travel plans, reconfirm.

In certain countries where inflation causes frequent changes in local prices or where the U.S. dollar is readily accepted, fares are quoted in U.S. dollars only.

## Acknowledgments

Many people have contributed to the completeness and accuracy of the listings. The author wishes to recognize the valuable assistance provided by the following:

**United States, Canada** C. M. Armour, Arthur E. Borchardt, James C. Parker, Jo-Ann Norris, Robert J. Larson, Robert Flannery, April Taylor, Louise Thomassin, Luanne Hoffman, B. Rapier, Gerald Vargas, Steven Goldman, Brad Christopher, Kevin Christ, Joseph Parnier, Denise Larscheid, Donna Norman, Janis Brand, Jon Satamoto, Madeleine Lasnier, Betsy Wade, Diane Wenger, Linden Cole, Ted Mathis, Fredric Cheikin, Eddie Storer, N. C. Merrill, Mark Oropeza, Frank Kamahele, Arthur Skelly, Tracy Lincoln, Karon K. Ellis, Betty Tozier, Larry Gould, and Robert Valance. And again this year, special thanks to O. H. (Jim) Schaller of Sunnyvale, Calif., retired United Airlines staffer, for all his help.

**Caribbean, Central & South America** Kelly Walsh, Barry Hutchinson, Arturo Eduardo Reyes, Antonio Ramos Mendiola, Myron Clement, Albert Chioda, Desiree Coffie, Emily Johnson, Laura H. Johnson, Tomas Polanco V., T. E. B. Oatham, Robert A. Smith, E. Ch. Michael Nicolaas, William Jedwab, Maria A. Ruiz de Sauma, Guillermo Bolanos, Jorge Palou Prietos Vicuna, Hector Perez Reyes, Jean Bozzuto, Leon Romero, Marcello E. L. Janzen, F. A. Arnell.

**Europe, Africa** Nicoline van der Velden, Kouabena Boko, Uwe Kirchneru, A. T. (Ted) Jumbe, Susanna Salo, Turgut

Kaya Yolsal, Dennis Droushiotis, Vladimir Kourkov, Alvaro de Sousa, Inge Uhrenbacher, Charles Thody, Carol Saunders, Nicos Velonis, Ellen Hoffman, Janine Lee, Annette Choynacki, Gedeon Furka, Hans Ley, Nils J. Flo, T. P. Haughey, Norman Bartlett, R. Facio, Aleksandar Vojnovic, William J. Boyd, Syrovy Hendrych, D. J. M. Dooley, A. Bridle, Muriel Lemaine, Wycliffe Wewa, Herman Gerns, S. K. Wamai, Richard Schano, Charles-Louis Roche, Georges Daverat, Olafur Ragnars, Stjepko Sarjanovic, Charles Treuhold, Svatopluk Rada, Abdullah H. Abdullkafe Ahmed, Fabrizio Rodriguez Pereira, Bjorn Hagner, Menachem Eyal, J. Stadler, Robin Prestage.

**Far East, Australia, New Zealand, Pacific** Rob Nelson, Alastair Paulin, George Francis, Chris Clarke, Peter Green, Carolyn Brown, Connie McNamara, Andrew Godi, Byoung Shik Rhee, M. Broadton, Ivor & Colleen Lewis, Kenneth Fischl, Asral Rapani, George Proos, Xie Gang, Qian Nai-Lin, Liu Yan-an, H. A. Coomer, John de Saram, Jose Jesus F. Roces.

Finally, special thanks to Abigail Crampton, who kept in touch with all our contributors—and kept the information flowing!

## Feedback

We rely on feedback from travelers to keep the listings current. If your experience differs from what is indicated here, or if you discover new options for getting away from the airport, please let us know. Our address is Airport to the City, P.O. Box 1214, Homewood, IL 60430.

Norman Crampton

## ABIDJAN, Ivory Coast
Aeroport Intl d'Abidjan-Port Bouet, 9.3 mi (15 km) SE

🚕 Hotel Ivoire CF1790 ($6), 30 min; Hilton and Novotel CF1430 ($4.70), 20 min. Fares are doubled between midnight and early morning.

🚗 Avis, Budget, Europcar, Hertz.

## ABU DHABI, United Arab Emirates
New Intl Airport, 12.5 mi (20 km) S

🚕 Di20-25 ($6-7.50), 20 min to city center. Di2 (60¢) each bag. Confirm fare with driver before you get in the cab. Tip 10%. Return fares from hotels slightly higher..

🚗 Avis, InterRent, National.

## ACAPULCO, Mexico
Juan N. Alvarez Airport, 12 mi (20 km) SE

🚕 $8, 30 min to La Condesa Beach area hotels.

🚐 Servicio Colectivo about every 10 min from 7 am to last flight. Stops anyplace on request along route through city. $3. Look for vehicle in front of terminal.

🚗 Avis, Dollar, Hertz, Sands.

## ADELAIDE, Australia
Adelaide Airport, 5 mi (8 km) W

🚕 A$7 ($5), 10-15 min.

🚐 Transit Coach Service from curb outside terminals every 30 min 6 am-9 pm to Hilton Intl, Richmond, other major hotels. A$1.50 ($1.05), 10-15 min.

🚗 Action, Avis, Budget, Hertz, Koala, Thrifty.

**P** A$6 ($4.20).

## AKRON-CANTON, Ohio

Akron-Canton Regional Airport, 15 mi SE of Akron, 10 mi NW of Canton

🚗 $12 flat rate, 15-20 min to Canton; $27 flat rate, 20-30 min to Akron. (If no cab at airport call Canton Yellow, 216-456-4343. May take 10 or more min to arrive.)

🚐 Hopkins Limousine to Quaker Square, Holiday Cascade downtown. Continues to Holiday Inn, Hilton in Fairlawn. $10.25. M-F at 5:15, 6:25, 7:35, 9:15, 10:30, 11:45 am; 1, 2:15, 3:30, 4:45, 6, 7:15 pm. Sun from 10:30 am. Sat-Hol 6:05 am, 12 noon only. Service also to Ramada Inn Northwest, Best Western Medina, Cleveland-Hopkins Airport. Info: 216-928-8172.

🚙 Avis, Budget, Dollar, Hertz, National, Snappy, Thrifty.

## ALBANY, Georgia

Albany-Dougherty County Airport, 4 mi SW

🚗 $4, 5-10 min.

🚙 Avis, Budget, Hertz, National.

**P** $2/day.

## ALBANY, New York

Albany County Airport, 10 mi NW

🚗 $9.90 flat rate; $6.40 each two or more. 18-20 min to Capitol.

🚐 Airport Limousine operates 6 am-12 am. $9.90 to Capitol. Reservations: 518-869-2258.

🚌 No. 1 Central bus every 30-60 min 5:43 am-6:07 pm. 60¢. 45-50 min run to Broadway, downtown.

🚙 Ajax, American Intl, Avis, Budget, Dollar, Hertz, National, Snappy, Thrifty.

# ALBUQUERQUE, New Mexico
Albuquerque Intl Airport, 5 mi SE

🚗 $6-8 + 12% fuel surcharge. Addl riders 35¢ each, 10-20 min.

🚐 Yellow Cab van, $8.

🚌 No. 50 bus every 30 min 6:37 am-6:07 pm M-F. Sat hourly 6 am-5 pm. No Sun, Hol. 30 min to Fifth & Gold, downtown, 60¢.

🚘 Alamo, American Intl, Avis, Budget, Dollar, Enterprise, Hertz, National, Snappy, Thrifty.

**To Santa Fe** See Shuttlejack listing at Santa Fe. Also Greyhound at 11:45 am, 3:45, 7:15 pm. **To Las Vegas, NM** TNM&O Airport Express at 11:30 am. $21. Info: 505-758-1144. Greyhound at 11:45 am. **To Espanola, Taos** Greyhound at 3:45, 7:15 pm. Greyhound Info: 505-243-4435.


# ALEXANDRIA, Louisiana
Esler Regional Airport, 15 mi NE

🚗 $7.50 flat rate, 25 min.

🚐 Airport Limousine meets flights, $7.50, 20 min.

🚘 Avis, Budget, National.

# ALICE SPRINGS, Australia
Alice Springs Airport, 9 mi (15 km) S

🚗 A$13-15 ($10.40-$12), 15 min.

🚐 Ansett Trailways, Alice Springs Airport & Railway Shuttle Service meet all arriving flights; A$4 ($3.20), 15 min.

13

🚗 Avis, Budget, Cheapa, Hertz, Thrifty.

**P** Free.

## ALLENTOWN, Pennsylvania
Allentown-Bethlehem-Easton Airport, 4 mi NE

🚕 $9, 15-20 min. To Bethlehem, $8-9, 20 min; to Easton, $25, 30 min.

🚗 Avis, Budget, Hertz, National.

## AMARILLO, Texas
Amarillo Intl Airport, 9 mi E

🚕 $11.90-$12.10, extra riders 50¢ each. 15-20 min.

🚗 Avis, Budget, Dollar, Hertz, National.

## AMSTERDAM, Netherlands
Amsterdam Airport Schiphol, 9 mi (15 km) SW

🚕 Dfl45-50 ($21.20-23.55), 20-25 min. To The Hague, Dfl110 ($52), 35 min; Rotterdam, Dfl145 ($68), 55 min; Utrecht, Dfl110 ($52). Cabs seat 4-6 persons. Meter fare includes tip but round up to next guilder for short ride, add 10% for longer hauls.

🚌 KLM Hotelline bus to nine major hotels every 30 min 5:55 am-9:45 pm, then 10:20, 11, 11:40 pm. Hilton Amsterdam, Barbizon, Park Apollo, others. Dfl12 ($5.65). Free to Ibis. 25-30 min. Good baggage space, comfortable.

🚆 To Amsterdam Centraal Station, every 15 min 5 am-12:05 am, then hourly. Dfl4.40 ($2.10), 17-20 min. Modern, comfortable cars, plenty of baggage space. Railway station is in basement, one level below arrivals area. Buy ticket before boarding. Schiphol is on the Dutch intercity rail network. Besides direct service to center city, World Trade, and RAI Convention Centre, express connections at Centraal station to Rotterdam, The Hague, Groningen, Leeuwarden, Flushing, and other points throughout Western Europe.

🚌 CN bus to RAI and Amstel stations every 30 min 6:24 am-6:24 pm, 7:03, 7:33 pm then hourly to 12:33 am. 57-67 min ride.

🚗 Ansa, Avis, Budget, Europcar, Hertz, Interrent, Olympic, Van Wijk.

**P** ST Dfl21 ($10), LT Dfl7 ($3.35). Longer term lot P3: Dfl25 ($12) first 5 days; thereafter, Dfl4.20 ($2)/day.

Schiphol sets the world standard for airport signage, both inside and outside the terminal.

## ANCHORAGE, Alaska
Anchorage Intl Airport, 5.5 mi SW

🚗 $12, 10-22 min.

🚐 ACE van every 15 min 5:30 am-midnight. $5. To Captain Cook, Anchorage Westward Hilton, Holiday Inn, Sheraton, other hotels. Also serves Palmer, Wasilla, Eagle River.

🚌 No. 6 People Mover from lower level hourly 7:20 am-7:50 pm M-F. 75¢. 20-25 min downtown.

🚗 Avis, Budget, Dollar, Hertz, National, Payless.

## ANGUILLA, Leeward Islands, West Indies
Wallblake Airport, 2 mi (3.2 km) SW of the Valley

🚗 To hotels: Malliouhana, 6-1/4 mi, $12 (US currency accepted); Cinnamon Reef, 2-1/2 mi, $7; Mariners, 3-1/2 mi, $8; Cove Castles, 8-1/2 mi, $15; Shoal Bay Villas,

4-1/2 mi, $8; Anguilla Great House, 8-1/2 mi, $10; Coccoloba, 9 mi, $15; Carimar Beach Resort, 7 mi $12; Rendezvous Bay Hotel, 8-1/2 mi, $10; Cap Juluca, 8 mi, $15.

🚗 Avis, Budget, Connors, H&R.

## ANKARA, Turkey
Esenboga Intl Airport, 18 mi (29 km) N

🚕 Tl9150 ($10) flat rate for up to 3 persons. 30-min.

🚌 Airport Bus operated by Turkish Airlines meets flights. $1.35 min.

🚗 Avis, Hertz, National.

## APPLETON, Wisconsin
Outagamie County Airport, 4 mi W

🚕 $6 flat rate one person, $1 each addl. 12 min.

🚗 Avis, Budget, Hertz, National.

P Free.

## ASHEVILLE, North Carolina
Asheville Regional Airport, 12 mi S

🚕 $15 flat rate, 15-20 min.

🚌 Blue Bird van to Asheville, $7.50, 15-20 min; to Hendersonville, $15, 15 min; to Black Mtn/Brevard, $25, 20 min; to Waynesville, $40, 35 min.

🚗 Avis, Budget, Hertz, National.

P ST $4.25, LT $3.25.

# ASPEN, Colorado
Aspen/Pitkin County Airport, 3-1/2 mi W

🚗 $8.05, 5-10 min; Snowmass, $12-14, 15 min; Highlands, $8-9, 10 min; Starwood, $10-12, 10 min. Addl passengers 50¢ ea; baggage 50¢ ea; airport departure fee 50¢.

🚌 Roaring Fork Transit Agency bus departs hourly 7 am-1 am during ski season from highway in front of terminal; 50¢; 5-10 min; baggage OK; less frequent service off season.

🚘 Avis, Budget, Eagle, Hertz, Mountain Express, National.

**P** ST $3.50, weekly $17.50.

# ATHENS, Greece
Hellinikon Airport, 6.5 mi (11 km) S

🚗 Dr800 ($5.30), 30 min downtown. Tip 10%. Dr25 (20¢) each bag. Double fare 1-5 am. Between terminals, a 7-min taxi ride. Also a bus every 20 min 6 am-midnight, Dr80 (55¢); midnight-6 am, Dr120 (80¢). Cabs not air conditioned.

## West Air Terminal, Olympic Airways

🚐 Olympic Airways bus every 30 min to city terminal on Syngrou Ave. Dr80 (55¢).

🚌 No. 133 from 6:10 am-12:30 am. Dr30 (20¢). 20-25 min to Syntagma (Constitution) Square. To Piraeus: No. 109 every 20 min 6 am-midnight. Dr30 (20¢).

## East Air Terminal

🚐 To Vassilisis Amalias Ave. every 20 min 6 am-midnight. Dr80 (55¢).

🚗 Avis, Budget, Hertz, InterRent/Batek.

**P** Dr140 (90¢).

## ATLANTA, Georgia
Atlanta Intl Airport, 8 mi SW

🚕 $13.50 flat rate one passenger, $7 each for two, $5 each for three. 20-30 min.

🚐 Atlanta Airport Shuttle every 20 min 5 am-midnight from ground transportation area. $7 OW $12 RT, 35-40 min to downtown hotels.

🚆 MARTA train from station next to baggage claim, South Terminal. Fare 85¢. Clean, quiet, air conditioned cars. Space to stow luggage and hang garment bags. Trains leave every 6-12 min, 5 am-1 am. 15-min ride to Five Points, downtown. Next stop, Peachtree Center, is a block or two walk from Ritz Carlton, Westin, Hyatt Regency, Barclay, Atlantan, Marriott, Best Western. Civic Center is the following stop, 17 min from airport.

🚗 Alamo, Avis, Budget, Dollar, General, Hertz, National.

**P** ST $12, LT $3.

**To Northern, Eastern Suburbs** Northside Airport Express daily every 45-60 min 6 am-12:15 am to Marietta/Windy Hill, Dunwoody, Chamblee-Tucker/Presidential, Gwinnett. Fares range $9.75-15 OW. Info: 404-455-1600. Roswell Airport Express hourly 6:45 am-11:30 pm to Crabapple Square. Info: 404-998-1893.


## ATLANTIC CITY, New Jersey
Atlantic City Intl Airport (Pomona Field), 13 mi NW

🚕 $22, 20 min.

🚐 Hotel vans meet arriving flights.

🚗 Avis, Budget, Hertz.

## ATLANTIC CITY, New Jersey
Bader Field, 1 mi W

🚗 $3.25, 5 min.

🚗 Avis, Budget, Hertz, Snappy.

## AUCKLAND, New Zealand
Auckland Intl Airport, 8.7 mi (14 km) N

🚗 NZ$32 ($21.25), 25 min. 10 pm-6 am and all day Sat, Sun, Hol: NZ$35 ($23.25). No tip.

🚐 Airporter from Intl terminal every 30 min 7 am-10 pm. Stops at domestic terminal, Travelodge, any bus stop en route, Sheraton-Auckland, Hyatt Kingsgate, Farthings hotels (opposite RR station). 35-40 min to last stop, downtown terminal. NZ$8 ($5.30) OW, NZ$14 ($9.30) RT.

🚐 Supershuttle operates 5 am-midnight (or last plane). NZ$8 ($5.30)

🚗 Avis, Budget, Hertz, Letz, National, Thrifty.

**P** NZ$10 ($6.65).

## AUSTIN, Texas
Robt. Mueller Municipal Airport, 4 mi NE of State Capitol

🚗 $5-$6, addl riders free, 8-9 min.

🚌 No. 12 bus at sign on center median outside baggage claim. Every 30 min M-F, every 30-60 min Sat-Sun. 50¢. 20 min to 6th & Colorado, downtown.

🚗 Avis, Budget, Dollar, Hertz, National.

# AYERS ROCK, Australia

Connellan Airport, 4 mi (6 km) N Yulara, 16 mi (26 km) NW Ayers Rock

🚌 Ayers Rock Touring meets flights; A$4 ($2.80), 10 min to Sheraton, Four Seasons, Campground, Lodge. To Ayers Rock: A$10 ($7), 20 min. To Mt. Olga: A$12 ($8.50), 40 min.

🚗 Avis, Budget, Hertz, Rock 'N' Ride, Thrifty.

# BAHRAIN ISLAND, Bahrain

Bahrain Intl Airport, Muharraq, 5 mi (8 km) NE

🚕 Sign posted at taxi ranks shows average fares to various destinations but expect to pay a little more. Across causeway to Manamah, D5 ($13.35), surcharge after midnight. No meters. Authorized cabs bear orange stripe; avoid others.

🚗 Arabous Car Hiring, Avis, Budget, Eurocar, Manzuri Transportation Service, Marsha Car Hiring.

# BAKERSFIELD, California

Meadows Field-Kern County Airport, 4 mi NW

🚕 $9, addl riders free. 10-15 min.

🚗 Avis, Budget, Hertz, National, Thrifty.

# BALI (Denpasar), Indonesia

Ngurah Rai Airport, 8 mi (13 km) SW

🚕 Cabs are blue. Higher fare is for A/C: to Denpasar, Rp6800 ($4), Rp 9000 ($5.40), 25 min; to Kuta Beach, Rp3200 ($2), Rp4500 ($2.70), 10 min; to Sanur Beach, Rp8700 ($5.20), Rp12,000 ($7.20), 25 min; to Nusa Dua Beach, Rp9200 ($5.50), Rp12,000 ($7.20), 20 min. Three-passenger limit to cab. Tip optional.

🚐 Some hotels provide free minibuses. Inquire.

🚗 Bali Happy, Bali Wisata at Kuta Beach. Intl license required.

**P** 12¢/day

## BALTIMORE, Maryland
Baltimore-Washington Intl Airport, 10 mi S

🚕 $12-14, 15-25 min to downtown Baltimore. Annapolis $25-27; Washington $35-40, 45 min.

🚐 BWI Airport bus/van, $5. Every 30 min 5 am-12:30 am M-F. Hourly Sat-Sun-Hol. Stops at downtown hotels. **To Annapolis 7 am-11 pm every 20 min. $12 OW, $22 RT.**

🚌 No. 16 Howard & Druid Hill bus at MTA sign, lower level. Inbound, M-F 6:45, 7:40, 8:21, 10:30 am; 4:42, 5:21, 6:01, 7:08 pm. Sat 8:31 am, 5:35 pm. No Sun. $1.15, 50-55 min ride to Charles & Lombard, downtown. **To National Airport, Washington** Airport Connection hourly from 5:15 am-9:15 pm, Sun-Fri. Sat every 2 hrs. Connection at Washington Capitol Hilton to Washington Flyer. $12, 70-80 min. Info: 301-859-3000.

🚗 Avis, Budget, Dollar, Hertz, National.

**P** ST $26, LT $7.

**To Amtrak** Free shuttle from airport to rail terminal 1.5 mi distant. Connections to Baltimore, Washington, New York. Info: 800-USA-RAIL and at Ground Transportation Counter, Central Terminal.

## BANGKOK, Thailand
Bangkok Intl Airport, 12 mi (20 km) N

🚖 Thai Intl Airways operates cabs marked by their logo. Flat rate about B300 ($12), no extras. No tip. A/C. Buy ticket at desk outside customs. 20-min trip.

🚌 Thai Airways bus to downtown air terminal every 20-30 min 6 am-midnight. Buy $3.50 ticket at Thai Limousine Service desk outside customs hall.

🚗 Avis, Hertz, Toyota.

## BANGOR, Maine
Bangor Intl Airport, 3 mi W

🚖 $4.35, addl riders 25¢ each, 8-10 min.

🚌 City Bus every 30 min 6:18 am-5:18 pm M-Sat. 60¢, 15 min. Flag bus down as it passes terminal.

🚗 Avis, Budget, Dollar, Hertz, National, Thrifty.

## BARCELONA, Spain
Barcelona Airport, 6 mi (10 km) SW

🚖 Pta1300 ($10.55), 15-20 min. Tip 10%.

🚆 RENFE train every 30 min 6 am-11 pm. Pay fare Pta89 (70¢) before boarding. Though station is half a mile from terminal, moving sidewalks make the connection easy. Follow pictograms. Roomy seats, plenty of baggage space. 16 min to Sants (Central) Station.

🚌 EA bus every 40 min 6:35 am-10:05 pm. Stops at yellow sign at either end of terminal. Fare Pta125 ($1) paid on board. 28 min to Plaza Espana, Metro connection. No baggage space, slow; but good way to see postwar sections of Barcelona.

🚗 Atesa/InterRent, Avis, Europcar, Hertz.

**P** Pta405 ($3.30)/day.

## BASEL, Switzerland
Basel/Mulhouse Airport, 6 mi (10 km) NW of Basel

🚕 SF12 ($8) to Hotel Schweizerhof, 15 min. To Mulhouse 20-30 min.

🚌 Swissair bus to Basel main railroad station. Pay fare SF4.60 ($3) Bus meets all flights. 15-20 min ride.

🚗 Avis, Budget, Europcar, Hertz, InterRent, Milleville.

P French side, F15 ($2.40). Swiss side, SF6 ($4).

## BATON ROUGE, Louisiana
Baton Rouge Metropolitan (Ryan Field), 8 mi NE

🚕 $12.50, 15-20 min.

🚗 Avis, Budget, Hertz, National, Snappy, Thrifty.

P ST $6, LT $4.50.

## BEIJING, China
Beijing Capital Airport, 18 mi (29 km) NE

🚕 RY25 ($8.40), 35-40 min. To Great Wall Hotel RY21 ($6), 30 min; Li Do Holiday Inn RY14 ($4), 20 min. No tip. English speaking taxi company is Capital Taxi, telephone 55-74-61. Be prepared to tell where you are located, where you are going.

🚌 CAAC (Civil Aviation Administration of China) bus to city ticket office RY2.70 (75¢). Meets flights. 40 min. It may be more convenient to take cab direct from airport rather than try to find one in city after leaving CAAC bus.

🚌 No. 359 bus from airport to Dongzhimen, center city. Every 10 min 5:10 am-9:30 pm, (10¢) 45 min.

🚗 Self-drive rentals not available in China. National Car Rental provides cars with drivers. Office: South Xin Hua Street, He Ping Men, Beijing. Tel: 33-13-49. Also, taxis always available in front of big hotels.

## BELFAST, Northern Ireland
Belfast Intl Airport, Aldergrove, 14 mi (22 km) NW

🚗 £9-12 ($14.50-19.30). £2 ($3.25) surcharge 11 pm-6:30 am.

🚌 Ulsterbus Express to main bus stations in Oxford and Great Victoria Sts. Every 30 min from 6:45 am M-Sat. Last, 10:10 pm. 7:15 am-10:15 pm Sun. Baggage space. Fare £2.50 ($4). 35-40 min trip. Follow "Way Out" signs from baggage claim, make right turn outside at "Bus and Taxi Rank" sign.

🚗 Avis, Godfrey Davis/Europcar, Hertz

**P** ST £15 ($24.15), LT £2 ($3.25)

## BELGRADE, Yugoslavia
Aerodrom Beograd, 10 mi (16 km) W

🚗 Din28000 ($5), to center city, RR station, JAT terminal. Baggage Din560 (10¢) ea. Tip 10%. 20-min ride.

🚌 Service every 15-20 min to Hotel Slavija, RR station, JAT terminal. Din4700 (85¢). 35 min.

🚗 AMSJ, Avis-Autotehna, Hertz-Kompas, Inex, Inter-Rent, Putnik, Unis.

**P** Din22400 ($4)/day.

## BERGEN, Norway
Bergen Airport, 11 mi (19km) SW

🚗 NKr160 ($24), 20 min. Tip 10%.

🚌 Meets arriving SAS and Braathens SAFE flights. NKr30 ($4.50); 30 min to bus terminal, then to Norge Hotel, SAS Royal Hotel. Return service every 30 min 5:50 am-9:20 pm. Outbound service starts at hotels, then picks up at bus terminal, where coaches may become crowded. Baggage racks.

🚗 Autohall, Avis, Budget/Tide, Hertz, InterRent, C. Seim Bilutleie.

**P** NKr25 ($3.70)/day.

## BERLIN, West Germany
Tegel Airport, 4 mi (7 km) NW

🚕 DM17-19 ($9-10.10). Tip 10%. DM1 (55¢) per bag.

🚌 No. 9 Airport City Bus from Gate 8, arrivals area. Also stops at upper level Main Hall. Leaves every 7-1/2 to 15 min 4:50 am-midnight. Fare DM2.70 ($1.45). Pay driver or use ticket-vending machine inside airport. 24-hr ticket can be purchased at airport or in city for DM9 ($4.80). Comfortable seating, baggage racks. Route into city is Kurfurstendamm. 30 min to Zoo—central train station for West Berlin. 8 min after leaving airport, bus stops at U-Bahn Jacob Kaiser Platz where bus ticket may be used as free transfer to U-Bahn, S-Bahn system.

🚗 Autohansa, Avis, Europcar, Hertz, InterRent, Sixt-Budget, Westfehling.

**P** ST DM12 ($6.40), LT DM7 ($3.80).

## BILLINGS, Montana
Billings Logan Intl Airport, 2 mi NW

🚕 $3 flat rate one person; $2.50 each two or more, 10 min.

🚗 Avis, Budget, Dollar, Hertz, National, Thrifty.

# BIRMINGHAM, Alabama

Birmingham Municipal Airport, 5 mi NE

🚗 $8-$9 one person, $5 each flat rate two or more, 15 min.

🚌 No. 20 Zion City bus. Every 30-45 min M-Sat, 6 am-6 pm. 80¢. 20 min run to 3rd Ave. & 21st St.

🚙 Avis, Budget, Dollar, Hertz, National, Payless, Snappy, Thrifty.

**P** ST $6.50, LT $3.


# BIRMINGHAM, England

Birmingham Intl Airport, 7 mi (11 km) SE

🚗 £6-8 ($10-13) downtown, 20-35 min. Tip 15%. There is a 25% surcharge for trips terminating more than 16 km from Birmingham center.

🚆 Air terminal is less than 1 km from British Rail's Birmingham Intl station. Good connections into Birmingham, other Midlands cities. Follow "Transit Link" signs first floor. Get aboard MAGLEV —departures every 5 min. 2-min ride to train station. Service to central Birmingham every 20 min 6 am-10 pm, then every 35 min until midnight. Sunday service about every 45 min. Fare 70p ($1.15). 15 min to Birmingham New Street, downtown. "Travel Centre" in rail station will help with other BritRail connections.

🚌 No. 58 West Midlands Travel from shelter at second curb outside terminal. Service about every 20 min 5:59 am M-F (6:42 am Sat) to 6:55 pm. Hourly 12:30-4:30 am with extra Sun departures at 5:30, 6:30 am—timings liable to alteration.

🚗 Avis, Godfrey Davis/Europcar, Hertz.

**P** ST £7 ($12), LT £1.85 ($3.20).

## BISMARCK, North Dakota
Bismarck Municipal Airport, 3 mi SE

🚕 $5, 10 min; extra passengers, $1 ea.

🚗 Avis, Budget, Hertz, National.

**P** $4/day.

## BOGOTA, Colombia
El Dorado Intl Airport, 8.5 mi (14 km) E

🚕 CP400 ($2), 30-40 min to city center. Police dispatcher gives passengers a ticket with fare to destination. This amount is paid to driver. Beware unlicensed cabs operating late at night after dispatch system closes.

🚗 Avis, Budget, Hertz, National.

## BOISE, Idaho
Boise Air Terminal, 3.5 mi S

🚕 $8, $1 extra for more than two riders. 10-15 min.

🚗 Avis, Budget, Dollar, Hertz, National, Payless, Thrifty.

## BOMBAY, India
Bombay Intl Airport, 19 mi (30 km) N

🚕 R105 ($7.40), 50-75 min. To Juhu Beach, R46 ($3.50), 25 min; to Dadar, R60 ($4.60), 35 min. Small bag, R3 (20¢), large bag, R5 (40¢). Four passengers maximum. Tip not expected.

🚌 Ex-Servicemen's Air Link Transport Service (EATS) on the hour from intl, domestic terminals except midnight, 1 am, 6 am. R25 ($1.75). 60 min ride to Air India Building, Nariman Point.

🚗 Not available in India.

**P** R8 (60¢)/day.


## BONN, West Germany See Cologne/Bonn, West Germany.


## BORDEAUX, France
Bordeaux (Merignac) Intl Airport, 8 mi (13 km) W

🚗 F70 ($11), 30 min. Fourth passenger (maximum load) pays F5 (80¢) addl. Baggage F2.60 each. Tip 10%.

🚐 Navette Aeroport coach hourly 6 am-10:45 pm M-F with hotel stops on demand on the way to Place Gambetta and Gare St. Jean. F26 ($4), 40 min. Sat service 6:10 am-9:15 pm; Sun 6:55 am-10:45 pm.

🚌 **To Merignac** CGFTE Bus No. 73 hourly 6:15 am-7:45 pm, Sun 7:50 am-7:40 pm. F12 ($2). Connects at Hotel des Postes with Service M to Bordeaux.

🚗 Avis, Budget, Citer, Europcar, Hertz, InterRent, Mattei, Milleville, Thrifty.

**P** ST F31 ($4.85), LT F26 ($4.10).


## BOSTON, Massachusetts
Logan Intl Airport, 3 mi NE

🚗 $10 to downtown Boston, Cambridge. 15-25 min. Share-a-Cab available at Terminal D 3:30-11 pm.

🚐 **Downtown** Airways red-white van hourly on the hour 8 am-10 pm to downtown hotels, $5.50. Up to hour travel time depending on traffic. Info: 617-267-2981. Also B&W Express, 617-426-8800.

🚌 **Framingham-Logan Express** Peter Pan bus leaves Logan every 30 min M-F 6:30 am-11 pm & 11:45 pm. Sat 7 am-11 pm on the hour. Sun 7 am-1 pm on the hour, 1:30 pm-11 pm every 30 min & 11:45 pm. 45-60 min to parking lot at Rte 30, Shoppers World, Framingham. Bus fare $7 OW, parking $4/day.

**Quincy/Adams-Logan Express** Plymouth & Brockton bus leaves Logan on same schedule as Framingham bus, above. 30-45 min to parking at MBTA station, Rtes 3 & 128. Bus fare $5 OW, parking (limited) $1.50/day.

🚁 HubExpress helicopter shuttle M-F 7 am-7 pm to & from regional heliports. To Hyatt Regency Cambridge at 7, 8:30 am; 5, 8 pm. Reservations: 800-962-4744.

🚊 Free bus No. 22 or 33 every 8-12 min to Airport Station of Rapid Transit (T). Clean, comfortable; baggage racks. At rail station, Blue Line train every 8-12 min 5:25 am-1 am. 60¢. Clean coaches, good wall maps. Four stops (20 min) to Government Center.

**Airport Water Shuttle** Free van every 15 min to Logan boat dock for water shuttle to Rowe's Wharf, next to Boston Harbor Hotel. Boat leaves every 15 min M-F 6 am-8 pm; every 30 min 12:15-7:45 pm Sat-Sun. $6. 7 min across harbor. Fine way to start the business day in Boston!

🚗 Alamo, American Intl, Avis, Budget, Dollar, Hertz, National.

**P** ST $48, LT $10.

**To South Shore/Cape Cod** Plymouth & Brockton Bus, 773-9400. Hudson Limo, 395-8080. **To SE Mass, Southern Suburbs** Bonanza Bus, 800-556-3815. Hudson Limo, 395-8080. **To Central Mass, Western Suburbs** Logan Express, 800-23-LOGAN. Hudson Limo, 395-8080. Quickway Airport Shuttle, 879-4788. **To N Central Mass, NW Suburbs** Hudson Limo, 395-8080. McCarty Limo, 800-233-0066. Townsend Limo, 597-6296. Vermont Transit Bus, 800-451-3292. **To N Mass, N Suburbs** Vermont Transit Bus, 800-451-3292. Marathon Shuttle, 603-898-2327. Hudson Limo 395-8080. Flight Line, 800-245-2525. **To N. Shore** C&J Airport Limo, 603-692-5111. Hudson Limo, 395-8080. **To New Hampshire** C&J Airport Limo, 603-692-5111. Concord Trailways Bus, 800-258-3722 (in Mass). Hudson Limo, 395-8080.

**Toll-free U.S. number for Logan Airport info: 800-23-LOGAN** At the airport, look for **information booths** opposite baggage claim in terminals A, C, E. Also interactive **video display terminals** nearby provide info 24 hours a day.


## BOZEMAN, Montana
Gallatin Field, 8 mi NW

🚕 Cabs do not wait at airport. Call 586-2341. $9 flat rate, 15 min. Extra passengers, $3 ea.

🚗 Avis, Budget, Hertz, National.

**P** $3.50/day.


## BRADENTON, Florida See SARASOTA/BRADENTON, Florida.

# BRATISLAVA, Czechoslovakia
Bratislava Ivanka Airport, 6 mi (10 km) NE

🚗 K100 ($4.20), 20 min. Tip 10%.

🚌 CSA-Bus meets arrivals, departures 6 am-midnight. Purchase ticket from driver, K5 (20¢). 30 min to city terminal near Hotel Palace, Devin.

🚌 No. 24 every 20 min 5 am-midnight from pick-up outside terminal. Pay driver K1 (5¢). 35 min to city. Baggage OK.

🚗 Avis, InterRent, Pragocar, Rent-Car.

P Free.


# BREMEN, West Germany
Bremen/Neuenland Airport, 2 mi (3-1/2 km) S ;DM12-15 ($6.50-8), 10 min.

🚃 No. 5 tram every 7-20 min 5:02 am-11:49 pm M-F. Sat-Sun service at 15-30 min intervals. DM2.4 ($1.30). To Bremen Hauptbahnhof in 15-20 min.

🚗 Avis, Europcar, Hertz, InterRent, Sixt Budget.

P DM6 ($3.25).


# BRIDGEPORT, Connecticut
Sikorsky Memorial Airport, 9 mi S

🚗 $10 flat rate, 12-15 min. To Fairfield $12-18, 20 min; Milford $12-22, 12-20 min; New Haven $28-41.50, 20-25 min.

🚌 Airport Taxi, $10. Operates 6 am-midnight. Door to door. Purchase ticket inside terminal. Suburban Limousine, reserve in advance: 203-377-8294.

🚗 Hertz.

**P** $5/day.

# BRIDGETOWN, Barbados
Grantley Adams Intl Airport, 9 mi (14.5 km) E

🚗 BD$26 ($14.35), 25 min. No tip necessary.

🚌 Barbados Transport bus boards directly opposite terminal on highway. Every 30 min 6 am-2 am. BD$1, 30 min to city center. Limited baggage only.

🚗 Avis, Dear's Garage (plus 31 other local companies— see classified phone directory)

**P** BD$4.50 ($2.50)/day

# BRISBANE, Australia
Brisbane Intl Airport, 7 mi (11 km) NE

🚗 A$9 ($7.20), 20 min.

🚐 Skennars Coaches meets flights. A$3.50 ($2.80), 20 min. Pay driver.

🚌 Brisbane City Council bus from Domestic Terminal every 35 min 6:15 am -11 pm. Sun every 2 hrs 9:15 am-7:15 pm. A$1 (70¢). 25-min ride.

🚗 Avis, Budget, Hertz, National, Thrifty.

**P** ST: A$12 ($8.50); LT A$6 ($4.25). Free shuttle every 15 min.

# BRUSSELS, Belgium
Brussels National Airport, 7.5 mi (12 km) NE

🚗 BF950 ($30), 20-30 min to city center. Metered fare includes tax, tip; make sure meter is on. RT ticket for BF1200 ($36) good for 2 months from Autolux taxis dis-

32

tinguished by small sign in top right corner windshield or back window.

🚆 Escalator to lower level entrance for train. Buy ticket BF72 ($1.90) at office. Penalty of BF600 ($15.60) for boarding train without ticket when office is open. Comfortable, plenty of baggage space. Trains every 30 min from 6:15 am. Last at 11:09 pm. 14 min to Brussels Nord, a Eurail transfer point; 18 min to Brussels Central, end of line.

🚗 Ansa, Avis, Budget, Continental, Europcar, Hertz, InterRent, Milleville, Toyota, Transcar, Travelcar.

**P** BF130 ($3.40)/day.

## BUCHAREST, Romania
Otopeni Intl Airport, 10 mi (16 km) N

🚌 City bus with special baggage compartment meets flights. Pay Leu8 (20¢) on boarding. 30-45 min ride to Tarom Airways headquarters in city where taxis are available.

🚗 ACR, Avis, ONT Carpati.

## BUDAPEST, Hungary
Ferihegy Airport, Terminal 1 (Intl), 10 mi (16 km) SE

🚕 Ft150 ($3), 20-30 min to city. Reserve cab at Volan Taxi counter next to rental cars. Flat rate includes service but a small tip will be appreciated. Malev flights arrive at more distant Terminal 2. Cab: Ft250 ($5), 30-40 min to city.

🚌 Volan Bus No. 1 to Engels Terrace, downtown. Bus leaves airport from stop at far right outside terminal.

Every 30 min 6 am-11:30 pm. Ft20 (40¢) to driver. Good baggage space, comfortable. From Terminal 2, Ft30.

🚌 No. 93 from far left as you exit terminal. 4:45 am-11:25 pm at 10-20 min frequencies. Purchase blue ticket from self-service machine inside terminal, on right as you head toward exit. Ft3 (6¢) for two tickets. Validate ticket in machine on bus. No baggage racks, limited floor space. But good chance you'll get a seat because airport is start of the route. To central Budapest, ride to end of bus line, transfer to M3 metro. Fare: Ft1 (2¢) into turnstile. Get off at Deak Terrace downtown. Total travel 50 min. Total cost 5¢! (Also picks up at Terminal 2.)

🚗 Avis/Ibusz, Europcar/Budget/Volantourist, Hertz-Fotaxi, InterRent.

## BUENOS AIRES, Argentina
Ezeiza Airport, 23 mi (37 km) SW

🚕 A$280 ($20.20), 30-40 min to downtown hotels. No extras, no tip.

🚐 Limo-type cars run by Manuel Tienda Leon. A$354 ($25.50) to center city. Drop you off anyplace, then to downtown bus station. Very comfortable.

🚌 Special bus from both terminals to downtown bus terminal, stopping at some hotels. Pay A$92 ($6.60) fare before boarding. 30-45 min trip.

🚗 Avis, Budget, Hertz, National.

## BUFFALO, New York
Buffalo Intl Airport, 8 mi NE

🚕 $13, 15-20 min.

🚐 Airport Taxi $5 to downtown hotels. Res: 716-633-8294.

🚌 No. 24A Genesee bus stops at East and West terminals. $1.10. 45-min ride to Lafayette Square.

🚗 American Intl, Avis, Budget, Hertz, National, Snappy, Thrifty.


## BURBANK, California
Burbank-Glendale-Pasadena Airport, 14 mi NW of Los Angeles

🚗 Burbank, $7-9; Glendale, $15-17; Pasadena, $25; downtown LA, $25-26. 25-45 min.

🚐 SuperShuttle to Burbank, Glendale, $10 first passenger, $6 each addl; Pasadena, $15. Info: 818-244-2700. Also, Prime Time. Info: 818-901-9901.

🚌 No. 94 RTD bus on island to right of terminal. $1.10 exact. Service every 20 min 5:16 am-12:47 am. Approx 1-hr ride to downtown LA. **To LAX** SuperShuttle, $11. Reservation a day in advance advised: 818-244-2700.

🚗 Avis, Dollar, Hertz, National.

P ST $18, LT $8. Remote $4, free shuttle.


## BURLINGTON, Vermont
Burlington Intl Airport, 3 mi E

🚗 $4.30 flat fare, addl riders $1 each. 10 min.

🚗 Avis, Budget, Dollar, Hertz, National, Thrifty.

# CAIRNS, Australia
Cairns Intl Airport, 4.5 mi (7.5 km) N

🚕 A$8 ($6.40), 10 min. To northern beach areas, 15-30 min. If no cab available use free phone or dial 515333. Tip not customary.

🚌 Airporter Shuttle Service (Garlen Coaches) meets flights. A$3.50 ($2.80) OW, A$6 ($4.80) RT. 10-20 min.

🚗 Avis, Budget, Hertz, Thrifty.

P A$4 ($3.20)/day.

# CAIRO, Egypt
Cairo Intl Airport, 9 mi (15 km) N

🚕 E£8-10 ($3.70-4.60) flat rate, 40-60 min. Disregard meter—determine fare in advance with driver. Tip E£1-2 (50¢-$1). Cabs not usually A/C.

🚌 Limo Bank Nasser. To Nile Hilton E£5 ($2.30); Gezira Sheraton E£8.5 ($3.90); Mena House E£10 ($4.60); Heliopolis E£4 ($1.85). Pay fare aboard. Stops at major hotels, other places on request. A/C. 45-70 min depending on route, traffic. Also goes to pyramids: inquire. Meets all flights.

🚗 Avis, Budget, Hertz, InterRent, National.

# CALCUTTA, India
Calcutta (Dum Dum) Airport, 17 mi (27.5 km) NE

🚕 R70-80 ($5.40-6.20), 60-70 min to city center.

🚌 Airport bus meets flights. R10 (80¢). Since a cab connection may be necessary from city terminal, it may be more convenient to take cab at airport.

🚗 Not available in India.

## CALGARY, Alberta

Calgary Intl Airport, 5 mi NE

🚕 C$15-16 ($10.50-11.20), 30 min downtown. To Calgary Olympic Center C$18 ($12.60), 35 min.

🚐 Airporter every 30 min 6:30 am-11:30 pm to Westin hotel. C$5 ($3.50) OW, C$8 ($5.60) RT.

🚌 No. 57 shuttle bus every 30 min 6:46-8:46 am; 12:16-10:57 pm. C$1.25 (90¢), get a transfer. Baggage OK. Change at Whitehorn Station (15 min) to train No. 202 downtown. 14 min to City Hall.

🚗 Avis, Budget, Dollar, Hertz, Thrifty, Tilden.

## CANBERRA, Australia

Canberra Airport, 3.5 mi (6 km) E

🚕 Cabs at airport peak times only. Telephone 460-444. A$7 ($5.60), 6-10 min. Woden, A$9 ($7.20), 15 min; Belconnen, A$12 ($9.60), 20 min; Tuggeranong, A$14 ($11.20), 25 min.

🚗 Avis, Budget, Hertz, Thrifty.

P Free.

## CANCUN, Mexico

Cancun Intl, 12 mi (20 km) SW

🚕 To hotel zone, $4.50; to city center, $3.75. Maximum 3 people.

🚐 To hotel zone in a combi (minibus), $1.50 per person for up to 5. 15 min.

🚗 Avis, Dollar Turisel, EconoRent Xelha, Hertz, National.

P $3.50/day.

**CANTON, Ohio** See Akron-Canton, Ohio.

## CAPE TOWN, South Africa
D.F. Malan Airport, 15 mi (23 km) NW

🚗 Rn36 ($14.05), 20 min. Tip 15%.

🚌 Interkaap bus meets every flight. Pay Rn6 ($2.40) aboard. Stops at South African Airways terminal in Cape Town. 25 min.

🚘 Avis, Budget, Imperial.

## CARACAS, Venezuela
Simon Bolivar (Maiquetia) Intl Airport, 13.6 mi (22 km) NW

🚗 $5, 35-40 min. Some airlines provide free transfer: inquire.

🚘 Avis, Budget, Hertz, National.

## CASABLANCA, Morocco
Nouasseur Airport, 22 mi (35 km) S

🚗 Dh100 ($15), 30 min. Tip $2.

🚌 CTM coach hourly on the hour from front of terminal. 40 min to city bus terminal.

🚘 Avis, Budget, Europcar, Hertz, Interloc, InterRent, Saudia, Safloc.

**P** $2/day

## CASPER, Wyoming
Natrona County Intl Airport, 8 mi NW

🚗 $8, 20 min; extra passengers, $2 each.

🚗 Avis, Budget, Hertz, National.

**P** ST $4, LT $2.75.

## CAYMAN BRAC, Cayman Islands
Gerrard-Smith Airport, 5 mi W

🚕 CI$6 flat rate, 10 min. Tip 10%.

🚗 Avis.

## CEDAR RAPIDS, Iowa
Cedar Rapids Municipal Airport, 8 mi S

🚕 $11.10, extra passengers 15¢ each. 10-15 min to Cedar Rapids.

🚐 DJs Limousine, $7-9 to Cedar Rapids; $10 OW, $18 RT to Iowa City. Look for desk at baggage claim. Meets flights.

🚗 Avis, Budget, Hertz, National, Thrifty.

## CHAMPAIGN/URBANA, Illinois
Univ. of Illinois-Willard Airport, 6.5 mi SW

🚕 $8-10, 20 min. Two or more passengers, $6 each.

🚗 Avis, Budget, Hertz, National.

**P** $4/day.

## CHARLESTON, South Carolina
Charleston Intl Airport, 12 mi NW

🚕 $12 flat for one or two passengers, $7.50 each addl, 20-25 min.

🚐 $7, 25 min. Reserve: 803-767-7111. AMEX, MC, Visa

🚗 American Intl, Avis, Budget, Dollar, Enterprise, Hertz, National, Snappy, Thrifty.

# CHARLESTON, West Virginia
Kanawha Airport, 4 mi NE

🚗 $7, 10-15 min.

🚘 Avis, Budget, Hertz, National, Thrifty.


# CHARLOTTE, North Carolina
Charlotte-Douglas Intl Airport, 8 mi W

🚗 $11 flat, each addl passenger $2. Bags 50¢. 15 min.

🚐 Yellow Cab Limousine, $4. 20-25 min to downtown hotels. Operates 7 am-11 pm. Call for Sat-Sun service: 704-332-6161.

🚘 Avis, Budget, Dollar, General, Hertz, National.

P ST $10, LT $3.


# CHATTANOOGA, Tennessee
Lovell Field, 10 mi E

🚗 $8 flat rate per person, 20-30 min.

🚌 No. 19 bus every 55 min. 75¢.

🚘 Avis, Budget, Dollar, Hertz, National, Thrifty.


# CHICAGO, Illinois
Meigs Field (lakefront), 2.3 mi SE of First Natl Bank Bldg in Loop

🚗 $4-6, 5-10 min to Loop, N. Michigan Ave. Cabs usually available weekdays. If not use cab phone at Butler Aviation desk.

🚘 None.

P Free. Limit 2 hrs.

# CHICAGO, Illinois
Midway Airport, 10 mi SW

🚕 $13-14, addl passengers 50¢ each. Share-Ride $8 to Loop. 20-40 min.

🚐 Airport Express vans every 30 min 8:30 am-8:30 pm M-F; to 5:30 pm Sat. Sun 11 am-8:30 pm. $7.50 OW, $13 RT. To Hilton, Palmer House, Marriott, Hyatt Regency, other hotels. 20-50 min. Res required for return: 312-454-7799. **South Suburbs** Tri-State Coach hourly 8:45 am-8:45 pm, then 9:20, 10:30, 11:40 pm to Oak Lawn, Alsip, Harvey, Homewood, Matteson, Lansing. Inquire about Indiana, Michigan connections. $10. Info: 312-374-7200. **To Hyde Park (U. of Chicago)** C.W. Airport Service at 8:30, 10:15 am; 12:20, 3:15, 6:15 pm for Best Roberts Motel, Ida Noyes Hall, Intl House, Windermere, Del Prado, Hyde Park Hilton. $7. Res: 312-493-2700. Boxes, bicycles, trunks, animals, $3.50 extra. **To LaPorte, Michigan City, Michiana Airport South Bend, Notre Dame, Mishawaka, Osceola, Elkhart** United Limo. Info: 800-833-5555.

🚌 No. 99M M-F rush hour bus picks up along Cicero Ave, just outside terminal. Service at 12-14 min intervals 6 am-8:15 am inbound, 4 pm-6 pm outbound. Via Stevenson Expy to State St Mall, downtown. $1. Often crowded and perhaps not best choice for travellers with much luggage. Transit to Midway will take great leap forward when rail link is finished in the early 1990s. **To O'Hare** C. W. Airport Service 6 am-9:45 pm at 1-2 hr intervals. $8.75. 45 min. Info: 312-493-2700. Tri-State Coach hourly 5:40 am-8:40 pm via Countryside. $10. 45 min. Info: 312-374-7200.

🚗 Avis, Budget, Dollar, Hertz, National.

**P** ST $10, LT $6.

# CHICAGO, Illinois

O'Hare Intl Airport, 18 mi NW

🚗 $19-20. Addl passengers 50¢ each. 25-60 min downtown depending on time of day. Share-a-Cab $12 each for three—may mean a short wait for full load. **To Midway Airport $32-35.**

🚌 Airport Express to downtown hotels $9.75 OW, $17 RT. Every 10-30 min 6 am-11:30 pm. **To Lincoln Park area** $8 OW, $15 RT. Every 30 min. **To North, NW Suburbs** Airport Express door-to-door to Evanston, Glencoe, Glenview, Highland Park, Kenilworth, Lincolnwood, Northbrook, Northfield, Skokie, Wilmette, Winnetka. $18, $4 for second passenger to same address. $9-10 to hotel stops. 6 am-11 pm daily. Res: 312-454-7799. Departs lower level outside baggage claim. **To South Suburbs, NW Indiana, SW Michigan** Tri-State Coach from lower level at United and between terminals 2 and 3. Hourly 6:35 am-8:35 pm to Alsip, Oak Lawn, Harvey, Homewood, Matteson, Lansing, Ill. 10:05, 11:20 pm, 12:35 am to Harvey only. $10, 45-70 min. To Hammond, Highland, Glen Park, Merrillville, Portage, Michigan City, Ind., hourly 6:15 am -12:30 am, $11-26. Connection to Stevensville, New Buffalo, Mich. 312-374-7200.

🚇 CTA subway-elevated train from terminal inside O'Hare direct to Loop (downtown) in 35-40 min. From baggage claim, follow rail-car signs down escalator or elevator to lower level, where moving sidewalks converge at station entrance. $1 fare to agent or exact coins in turnstile. Trains every 3-5 min peak hours, up to 30 min late night. 24-hr service. Baggage racks on some cars, some floor space. May be tight squeeze in rush hours. Trains, stations fairly clean. Loop platforms crowded in rush hours and could be better lighted. Travelers with little luggage and bound for central business district will find the O'Hare subway an excellent choice. During rush hours it often makes better time than cabs, limos. Airline employees are among regular riders. **To Midway** C.W. van 8:30 am-10:45 pm every 1-2 hrs. $8.75, 45 min. Info: 312-493-2700. Tri-State Coach via Countryside. Hourly 7:10 am-10:10 pm. $10, 45 min. Info: 312-374-7200.

🚗 Airways, Avis, Budget, Dollar, Hertz, National, Payless, Snappy, Thrifty.

**P** ST $12, LT $6. Free shuttle.

All the following board from lower level between terminals 2 & 3: **To Hyde Park (U.of Chicago)** C.W. Limousine every 45-60 min. $8.50. Stops at Lake Meadows, Hyde Park Hilton, Windermere, Del Prado, Intl House, Ida Noyes Hall, Best Roberts Motel. 312-493-2700. **To Naperville, Lisle, Aurora** Airtran 312-961-5500. **To Madison, Janesville, Beloit** Van Galder Alco 312-253-0066. Greyhound 608-257-0440. **To Rockford, Freeport, Monroe (Wis)** Van Galder Alco 312-253-0066. **To Lake Geneva** O'Hare Wisconsin Limousine (OWL) Serv. 312-427-3102. **To Rockford, Peoria** Peoria-Rockford Bus Co. 309-688-9523 **To Joliet, Dwight, Pontiac, Normal, Bloomington, Ottawa, Morris, LaSalle, Peru** Prairieland Shuttle 800-322-6546 (Illinois) 800-882-0082 (US) **To LaPorte, South Bend, Mishawaka, Elkhart, Ind.** United Limo 800-832-7323 (Indiana) 800-833-5555 (US) **To Deerfield, Lake Forest, Waukegan Continental Air Transport 312-454-7799.**

**To Mitchell Field, Milwaukee** Greyhound from bus dock at curb between terminals 2 & 3 at 12:20, 5:40, 9, 11:30 am; 1:15, 2:15, 3, 4:15, 5:15, 6:15, 8, 9:45 pm. $9 OW, $15 RT. 1 hr 45 min trip. Info: 414-272-2954. Also United Limo at 7:30, 9, 11 am; 1, 3, 5, 7:30, 10 pm. $10 OW, $15 RT. Info: 414-747-1666.

## CHIHUAHUA, Mexico
Genl Roberto Fierro Villalobos Airport, 11 mi (17.6 km) NE

🚎 To Center City, P2950 ($1.30); residences, P8150 $3.60.

🚗 Ansa, Avis, Budget, Fast, Hertz, National.

**P** $6.30/day.

## CHRISTCHURCH, New Zealand
Christchurch Intl Airport, 7 mi (11 km) NW

🚗 NZ$14 ($9.30), 10 min. To Governor's Bay NZ$20 ($13.30), 30 min. No tip.

🚌 Airport bus about every 30 min 6:35 am-10:15 pm M-F.Sat from 7:17 am. Limited service Sun, Good Friday, Christmas Day. 30 min to city, NZ$3 ($2).

🚗 Avis, Budget, Hertz.

## CINCINNATI, Ohio
Greater Cincinnati Intl Airport, 13 mi SW

🚗 $20 flat. 20-30 min.

🚎 Jet Port Express every 30 min 6 am (8 am Sat-Sun)-11:30 pm to Westin, Hilton, Clarion, Hyatt Regency, Netherland Plaza. $8 OW, $11 RT. 30 min to city.

🚗 Avis, Budget, Dollar, Hertz, National.

**P** ST $4.50, LT $2.50.

## CLEVELAND, Ohio
Cleveland-Hopkins Intl Airport, 10 mi SW

🚗 $16, 20-35 min to Public Square, downtown

🚎 Hopkins Airport Limo to North Randall, Shaker

Heights, Beachwood, Solon, Wilson Mills, Oberlin, Elyria, Kent U., and vicinity. Info: 216-267-8282.

🚃 Airport/Windermere train from station inside air terminal Every 10 min rush hours, 15-30 min other times. 4:30 am-12:20 am daily. Runs at 20-30 min intervals Sun-Hol. $1. 22 min to Cleveland Union Terminal (Public Square), downtown. Clean, bright coaches and stations, ample baggage space.

**To Akron-Canton Airport** Hopkins Airport Limo every 75 min 7 am-10:30 pm M-F, stopping at Best Western Medina, Ramada Inn NW, Holiday Inn, Hilton, Fairlawn, Holiday Cascade, Quaker Sq. Hilton. $12.75. Info: 216-267-8282

🚗 Avis, Budget, Dollar, Hertz, National, Snappy, Thrifty.

**P** ST $8, LT $4.

# COLOGNE/BONN, West Germany
Cologne/Bonn Airport, 8.7 mi (14 km) SE of Cologne, 12 mi (20 km) NE of Bonn.

🚕 To Cologne, DM30 ($16.25), 20 min; to Bonn, DM46 ($25), 25 min. To Aachen, DM145 ($79), 1 hr; to Wuppertal, DM115 ($62), 1 hr; to Leverkusen, DM45 ($24.50), 35 min. Tip 10%.

🚐 To Cologne, Line 170 coach from arrival level departs at 20-30 min intervals 6 am-11 pm, 20 min to city. Pay driver DM6 ($3.25). To Bonn, Bonn Line FL departs every 30 min 5:40 am-11 pm, 25 min to city. Pay driver DM6 ($3.25).

🚗 Autohansa, Avis, Europcar, Hertz, InterRent, Hans Sixt.

**P** ST DM10 ($5.40), LT DM5.20 ($2.80). In the Parkplatz Nord lot, parking is free for passengers departing on holidays of at least 1 week.

## COLOMBO, Sri Lanka
Katunoyake Intl Airport, 20 mi (32 km) N

🚕 Rs275 ($13.50), 50 min. Buy ticket at taxi counter. Look for "Airport Taxi" sticker on windshield. To Kandy (Hill capital), Rs875 ($43.15), 2 hrs; to Anuradhapura (ancient city), Rs1560 ($77), 5 hrs; to Hikkaduwa (beach resort), Rs1050 ($52), 3.5 hrs. No tip expected but Rs10-20 will be appreciated on Colombo run, more on longer jaunts.

🚐 Coach leaves from car park opposite terminal every 30 min from dawn to late night. Rs4 (15¢), 60 min to main bus stop in Colombo.

🚌 Sri Lanka Transport Board operates service to Kandy: Rs10 (36¢), 3 hrs; and Negombo: Rs3 (10¢), 20 min. Inquire at taxi counter.

🚗 Avis, Europcar, Hertz, National.

**P** Rs10 (50¢)/day.

## COLORADO SPRINGS, Colorado
Colorado Springs Municipal Airport, 8 mi SE

🚕 $9.50 downtown, Broadmoor Hotel $13.50. 15-20 min.

🚐 Airport Transportation Service. To downtown $5.50, Broadmoor $6.

🚗 Avis, Budget, Dollar, Enterprise, Hertz, National, Payless, Thrifty.

## COLUMBIA, South Carolina
Columbia Metropolitan Airport, 6 mi SW

🚗 $10 for one or two, 50¢ each addl passenger. 10-15 min.

🚙 Avis, Budget, Dollar, Enterprise, Hertz, National, Snappy, Thrifty.

## COLUMBUS, Georgia
Columbus Metropolitan Airport, 5 mi NE

🚗 $8, 10 min. To Ft. Benning, $17, 20 min. Extra passengers, 50¢ each. Baggage, 50¢ each.

🚙 Avis, Budget, Hertz, National.

**P** ST $5/day, LT $3/day.

## COLUMBUS, Ohio
Port Columbus Intl Airport, 7 mi E

🚗 $10-11, 20 min.

🚌 Airport Limo every 30 min 7 am-11:10 pm. Sun from 3 pm. $5.25 OW, $9.50 RT. To Holiday Inn, Christopher, Sheraton, Hyatt, Hyatt Capitol, Great Southern, Pickett Suites, Victorian Inn, bus station.

🚙 Avis, Budget, Dollar, Hertz, National.

**P** ST $16, LT $8, Remote $4.50.

## COPENHAGEN, Denmark
Copenhagen Airport, 6.25 mi (10 km) SE

🚗 DKr90 ($12.50), tip incl; 15-20 min. Metered taxis with signs atop.

🚌 SAS bus, DKr24 ($3.40), from outside arrival hall to Hotel Scandinavia, Central RR Stn. Departures every

15 min from 5:45 am. Last at 11:10 pm. Baggage racks. 25-30 min ride.

🚌 Bus No. 32 from outside arrivals hall. Pay DKr10 ($1.50) when boarding. Departures every 10-20 min 4:31 am-11:48 pm. 30-45 min to Town Hall Square. Little baggage space, 20 stops into city. After-hours service available but requires transfer; ask driver. First bus Sun 5:22 am.

**To Malmo, Sweden** Bus from airport to water landing, then hydrofoil or hovercraft across Sound to Malmo. Summer departures hourly 6:20 am-8:20 pm, then every 30 min to 12:20 am, then 1:20, 2:20, 2:50 am. Hourly evening service in winter. 35 min.

🚗 Avis, Budget, Eurocar, Hertz, InterRent, Pitzner.

**P** ST DKr35 ($5), LT DKr15 ($2.15).

## COZUMEL ISLAND, Mexico
Cozumel Airport, 1.9 mi (3 km) N

🚗 $3, 5-10 min.

🚐 Servicio Colectivo from front of terminal every 10 min 7 am to last flight. 10 min; 75¢.

🚗 Avis, Budget, Hertz.

## DALLAS, Texas
Dallas Love Field, 7 mi NW

🚗 $10, addl passengers 50¢ each. 15-25 min.

🚐 SuperShuttle vans to downtown, Market Center hotels every 30 min M-F, hourly Sat-Sun. $7. Wait outside baggage claim to flag van as it rolls through.

🚌 DART No. 39 Love Field bus at 10 min intervals peak times, 30-40 min other times. 5:28 am-10:31 pm. 75¢

exact. Approx 35 min to Lamar & Main, downtown. Take return bus along Commerce St.

🚗 Avis, Budget, Hertz, National.

# DALLAS-FT. WORTH, Texas

Dallas-Ft. Worth Airport, 21 mi NW of Dallas, 24 mi NE of Ft. Worth

🚕 **To Dallas**, $20 flat fare plus extras: 50¢ airport toll; 50¢ each extra passenger 7 am-7 pm, $1, 7 pm-7 am; $3 surcharge midnight-6 am. Transfer between terminals, $5. Minimum fare leaving airport $10. 25-40 min to downtown Dallas. **To Ft. Worth**: $22 flat fare, same addl charges as above. 30-40 min.

🚐 **To Dallas** TBS, VIP vans to downtown, Market Center hotels including Hilton, Sheraton, Plaza of the Americas, Fairmont, Greenleaf, Adolphus, Holiday Inn, Hyatt Regency, Anatole, Marriott Market Center, Wyndham, Viscount. $8-10, 45-60 min. Info: Use courtesy phone. Departures every 30-60 min 8:20 am-9:20 pm. **To Ft. Worth** "T" Bus at 5:55 am, then hourly 7:10 am-7:10 pm, then 8:04, 9:04, 10:04, 11:05 pm. To Day's Inn, Greyhound, Hyatt, Hilton, Ramada. $6. A 50-70 min ride after leaving Terminal 4E.

🚐 **To Dallas/Ft. Worth** SuperShuttle vans to downtown Dallas hotels, $8. Other downtown locations, $10 first passenger/$6 each addl. To N. Dallas/Galleria $15/$7; Irving $10/$7; Arlington $10/$6; Richardson $18/$7; Plano $20/$8; E. Dallas $15/$7; Ft. Worth $18/$7. Departures every 15-30 min throughout the day, on call 24 hours. Info: 817-329-2020. AMEX, MC, VISA.

**American Airlines Park-and-Ride** AAirlink from Dallas parking lot at LBJ Fwy (I-635) & Midway Road. Park free, take SuperShuttle to DFW. $11. 30-40 min. AAirlink from Ft. Worth parking lot at Green Oaks Inn, W side business district. Park free, take SuperShuttle to DFW. $15. 40 min. SuperShuttle schedule geared to AA departures, arrivals.

🚗 Alamo, Avis, Budget, General, Hertz, National, Thrifty. No counters in terminal. Use phone in baggage claim or watch for courtesy van outside baggage claim.

**P** ST $10, LT $4. Free shuttle.

**To Plano** Texas Transportation at 12:05, 1:50, 3:35, 5:05, 6:05, 6:50, 9:05 pm. To hotels, $15 first passenger, each addl $8. To other addresses, $20 first passenger, $8 each addl. **To NE Texas** NE Texas Flyer to Paris $30 OW, $50 RT; Sulphur Springs $28 OW, $46 RT; Greenville, $22 OW, $37 RT. Info: 800-327-3265. **To Waco** The Streak at 10 am, 12:30, 3, 5:30, 8 pm. $25 OW, $40 RT to Hillsboro; $30 OW, $50 RT to Waco hotels, Baylor. **To Wichita Falls** Skylark Van Service at 9:15 am, 12:15, 3:15, 8:15 pm. $25/$45. Res:817-322-1352.

# DARWIN, Australia
Darwin Airport, 4 mi (7 km) NE

🚗 A$7 ($5.60), 10-15 min. To Nightcliff, A$6 ($4.80), 10 min; Woodleigh Gardens, A$9.50 ($7.60), 15 min. Tip not customary but A$1 OK.

🚐 Darwin Airport Services meets flights, drops off at hotels, motels throughout city. A$3 ($2.10). Buy ticket at Tourist Information Centre.

🚗 Avis, Budget, Cheapa, Hertz, Letz, Territory Truck, Thrifty.

**P** Free.

# DAYTON, Ohio
Dayton Intl Airport, 12.5 mi N

🚗 $13.50, 20¢ each addl passenger. 15-20 min.

🚐 Airport Limo every 40 min 5:45 am-11:25 pm. $7 OW, $13 RT. 20-25 min to Marriott, Dayton Plaza, Hilton, Belton Inn, Ramada, Stouffer Inn. Weekends by reservation: 513-898-7171.

🚙 American Intl, Avis, Budget, Dollar, Hertz, National, Snappy, Thrifty.

# DAYTONA BEACH, Florida
Daytona Beach Regional Airport, 3 mi SW

🚗 $14, 50¢ each addl rider. 15-20 min.

🚙 Avis, Budget, Dollar, Hertz, National.

# DELHI, India
Palam Airport, 10 mi (16 km) W

🚗 R60 ($4.65), 40-45 min. Atel cabs, yellow and black, are metered. Make sure meter is running. No tip expected. Baggage R5-10 (40-80¢) apiece. Not A/C. For A/C comfort, inquire at Ashok Travel and Tour desk to reserve car and driver. R134-168 ($10.30-13) flat rates. 30-40 min into city.

🚐 PTC (Pallavan Transport Corporation) coach from domestic and intl terminals. Meets flights. Pay R15 fare ($1.15) to driver. Stops at major hotels, Egmore RR station on way to Indian Airlines office in Connaught Place, city center. 40-60 min.

🚌 PTC bus from near Intl terminal to Connaught Place. Every 30 min 5:30 am-9:30 pm. Many stops along way, no special room for baggage, not A/C. Fare, paid aboard, R1.5 (8¢). 60-min ride.

🚊 PTC train every 10 min 4:30 am-11:30 pm. Baggage space. R2 (16¢). 45 min.

🚗 Not available in India.

## DENVER, Colorado
Stapleton Intl Airport, 7 mi NE

**Toll free US number for Denver airport ground transportation info: 800-AIR-2-DEN.**

🚕 To downtown hotels, $8-9, 15-20 min. 40¢ each addl passenger, 50¢ airport gate fee. Tech Center $14-22; Aurora area $6-16; Lakewood-West $17-21; Lakewood-Southwest $18-21; Northglenn $20-22; Littleton $19-25; Englewood $15-17; Boulder $36-40. Ski areas: Steamboat $204; Winter Park $94; Vail $132; Aspen $264.

🚐 Van every 15 min M-F, 30-45 min Sat-Sun, to Brown Palace, Radisson, Holiday Inn, Fairmont, Executive Towers, Westin, Embassy Suites, Marriott. $5. 20-25 min downtown. Buy ticket at Airporter counter in Ground Transportation Center, lower level opposite Door 6. **To Boulder** Boulder Airporter hourly 9 am-10:15 pm. 40-min run to Boulderado Hotel, Clarion, Broker Inn. $8.

**To other Denver-area locations** Call toll-free 800-AIR-2-DEN or inquire at Ground Transportation Center. Many scheduled and unscheduled services link Stapleton Airport and points in metro Denver; Ft. Collins; Cheyenne and Laramie, Wyoming; Scotts Bluff, Nebraska; ski/resort areas; military installations.

🚌 No. AB express bus to Denver, Boulder. 7:10, 8:10 am then every 30 min to 2:40 pm; then 3:12, 3:37, 4:07,

4:37, 5:07, 5:52 pm; then hourly 6:40 pm-12:40 am. Sat hourly from 6:40 am. Sun-Hol hourly from 7:40 am. Fare to driver: $1.25 Denver, $2 Boulder. Baggage OK, bicycles if space available. 20 min to Denver Bus Center (20th & Curtis); 80 min to Boulder Transit Center (14th & Walnut). Also No. 32 bus 4:51 am-12:44 am M-F at 15-min intervals 6-9 am, 30 min other times. Board at Red Zone, outside Door 11. 75¢ exact. 23 min to 17th & California, downtown. Operates 5 am-12:44 am Sat-Sun at 30-min intervals. **To Colorado Springs** Airline Connection at 8:30, 10:55 am; 1, 5, 8, 10:45 pm via Sheraton, Clarion hotels to Colo Spgs Airport. Continuing service to Pueblo. $20 to Colo Spgs, $30 to Pueblo. Res, Info: 800-288-2227.

🚗 Alamo, American Intl, Avis, Budget, Dollar, General, Hertz, National, Payless, Snappy, Thrifty, Western.

**P** First 30 min free all lots. Then ST $24, LT $3. SMART shuttle all hours every 10 min.

## DES MOINES, Iowa
Des Moines Intl Airport, 5.5 mi SW

🚕 $7-8, 50¢ each addl rider. 15-20 min.

🚌 No. 8 bus from Frontage Road hourly 6:50-11:50 am, 1:18-5:53 pm. 60¢.

🚗 Avis, Budget, Dollar, Hertz, National.

## DETROIT, Michigan
Detroit City Airport, 6.5 mi NE

🚕 $11, 15-30 min.

🚐 Commuter Transportation Co. vans at 9, 11:30 am; 12:30, 1:30, 2:30, 3:30, 5:30, 6:30, 7:30, 8:30, 9:30, 11 pm, midnight. To St. Regis, Day's Inn, Pontchartrain, Cobo Hall, Omni, Westin, Shorecrest. $5. **Mt. Clemens** Holiday Inn, $13; **Roseville** Georgian Inn, $8; **Harper Woods** Park Crest, $8; **Troy** Somerset Inn, Hilton, $12; **Hazel Park** Holiday Inn, $10; **Warren** Sterling Inn, Van Dyke Park Place, $10. AMEX, MC, Visa.

**To Detroit Metro. Wayne County Airport** Commuter Transportation Co. vans hourly. $12. AMEX, MC, Visa.

🚗 Hertz, National.

**P** ST $9. LT $5, $25/week.

# DETROIT, Michigan
Detroit Metro. Wayne County Airport, 19 mi SW

🚗 $28, 30-45 min to downtown Detroit. Romulus $10.20; Southfield $30.80; East Detroit $37.50; Ann Arbor $34.80; Dearborn $18.40; Pontiac $41.90.

🚐 Commuter Transportation Co. vans every 30 min 7:15 am-midnight M-F, hourly on the hour Sat-Sun. $11 OW, $20 RT. To Westin, Omni, Cobo Hall, Leland, Pontchartrain, Days Inn. **To Dearborn** Hourly 7:15 am-11:15 pm to Holiday Inn Fairlane, Hyatt Regency, Dearborn Inn, Dearborn Holiday Inn. $8 OW, $14 RT. **To Southfield** Hourly 7 am-midnight. $15 OW, $28 RT. Also service to: New Center, St. Regis, Grosse Pointe, Fraser, Warren (including GM Tech Center), Roseville, Farmington Hills, Novi, Livonia, Plymouth, Rochester, Troy, Hazel Park, Ypsilanti, Ann Arbor. Info & Res: 800-458-9401 (US), 800-351-LIMO (Mich). AMEX, MC, Visa.

**To Detroit City Airport** Commuter Transportation Co. vans hourly on the hour 7 am - midnight. $12. 30-45 min.

🚗 Alamo, Avis, Budget, Dollar, Hertz, Holiday Payless, National, Snappy, Thrifty.

**P** ST $16, LT $2.50. Free shuttle every 10-12 min.

## DUBAI, United Arab Emirates
Dubai Intl Airport, 10 mi (16 km) N

🚕 Di30 ($8), pay in advance at taxi desk. Bags Di2 (55¢) each. Pleasant 15-20 min ride on oceanside road. To Abu Dhabi Di200-250 ($55-70).

🚗 Avis, National.

## DUBLIN, Ireland
Dublin Airport, 5.5 mi (9 km) N

🚕 I£7.50 ($12), 20-30 min to Buswell's Hotel. Extra riders 40p (65¢) ea. Baggage 40p (65¢) ea. Tip 10%.

🚐 Airport Service from Arrivals Terminal at 35 min intervals 8:10 am-9:25 pm. Pay driver I£2.30 ($3.70). Approx 25 min to Gresham, Skylon hotels, Store St. bus terminal.

🚌 No. 41A boards at bus stop, a short walk from arrivals hall. Departures about every 30 min 6:10 am-11:20 pm. Pay driver 90p ($1.40). Double-deckers have small amount of storage space beneath stairs. 30 min to Eden Quay, many stops en route. Buses No. 41, 41C also at peak times. For traveler with little luggage, this can be a delightful top-deck trip into town.

🚗 Avis, Budget, Europcar, Hertz, Johnson & Perrott, Murrays.

**P** ST I£5 ($8), LT I£2.40 ($3.80).

## DUNEDIN, New Zealand
Dunedin Airport, 18.6 mi (30 km) SW

🚗 NZ$35 ($23), 30-35 min. Cabs not always at airport; use free taxi phone. To Port Chalmers Wharf NZ$44 ($29), 60 min; Queenstown NZ$320 ($212), 3 hrs; Alexandra NZ$210 ($139), 2 hrs; Invercargill NZ$247 ($164), 2 hrs 10 min. No tip.

🚌 Ritchies Coachlines meets flights. NZ$8 ($5.30), 30-35 min to High St. & Octagon, city center.

🚗 Avis, Budget, Hertz.

## DURHAM, North Carolina See RALEIGH/ DURHAM, North Carolina.

## DUSSELDORF, West Germany
Dusseldorf Airport, 5 mi (8 km) N

🚗 DM20 ($12), 15 min. Tip 5%.

🚌 Bus 727 to Hauptbahnhof (main central station) every 20-30 min 5:30 am-midnight. Boards on arrivals level outside taxi ranks. Comfortable, plenty of baggage space. DM2.60 ($1.30). 22 min.

🚊 S-Bahn No. 7. Follow signs from baggage claim to lower-level terminal. Long tunnel connects to rail station but luggage conveyor belt makes transfer somewhat easier. Self-service ticket machine dispenses zone fare cards. Two zones to Hauptbahnhof, downtown, costs DM2.60 ($1.30). Tickets must be cancelled at validating machine before boarding. Trains every 20 min 5:03 am -12:03 am. Plenty of luggage space, A/C. 12-min ride.

🚗 Autohansa, Avis, Europcar, Hertz, InterRent, Sixt-Budget.

**P** ST DM64.80 ($34.40), LT DM4-DM13 ($2.20-$7.20) depending on location. There are 10 garages or lots with a total capacity of 14,000.

## EDINBURGH, Scotland
Edinburgh Airport, 7 mi (11 km) W

🚕 £7 ($11.30), 15-25 min. Cabs say Airport Taxi. They are metered and take up to four people. No extra charges. Tip 15%. Look for taxi rank near Door D between gates 3 and 4.

🚐 No scheduled service but Crest Hotel, Royal Scot Hotel operate courtesy coaches.

🚌 Airlink No. 100 departs from bus stop outside Door D. No special baggage space. Departs every 30 min 6:05 am-10:35 pm except Sat-Sun when service is hourly. No service Christmas, New Year's days. Pay £1.65 ($2.65) on bus. Stops at Ingliston, Maybury/Royal Scot Hotel, Drum Brae, Zoo, Murrayfield, Haymarket, West End, Waverley Station. 25-30 min ride.

🚗 Avis, Europcar, Hertz, Swan National.

**P** £3.50 ($6)/day first 6 days; £2.50 ($4.30) each day thereafter.

## EDMONTON, Alberta
Edmonton Intl Airport, 15 mi S

🚕 C$25 ($19), 30 min.

🚐 Grey Goose Airporter every 20 min 6:20 am-1 am M-F. Hourly Sat-Sun. C$7 ($5.25) OW, C$12 ($9) RT. Serves Westin, Four Seasons, Chateau Lacombe, Sheraton, and other hotels.

🚗 Avis, Budget, Hertz, Holiday, Tilden.

## EL PASO, Texas
El Paso Intl Airport, 5 mi E

🚗 $14, 50¢ each addl rider. 15-20 min.

🚐 Sprint van every 15 min. $9 downtown, $10 Ft. Bliss, $12 West Side.

🚗 Avis, Budget, Dollar, Hertz, National.

## EVANSVILLE, Indiana
Evansville Dress Regional Airport, 3 mi N

🚗 $9, 25¢ each addl passenger. 15 min.

🚌 METS Airport bus from front of terminal hourly M-Sat 6:45 am-5:45 pm. 50¢ exact fare. 30 min downtown.

🚗 Avis, Budget, Hertz, National, Thrifty.

**P** ST $8, LT $3.50.

## FAIRBANKS, Alaska
Fairbanks Intl Airport, 7 mi W

🚗 $7.50, addl passengers $1 each. 15 min.

🚐 Most hotels provide a courtesy van or will reimburse cab fare.

🚗 Avis, Budget, Hertz, National, Payless, Rainbow.

## FARGO, North Dakota
Hector Intl Airport, 3 mi NW

🚗 Cabs do not wait at airport. Look for phone in vestibule. $7-8, 10 min. To hotels in S. Fargo, $7-10, 10-15 min. Extra passengers 50¢ ea.

🚗 Avis, Budget, Hertz, National, Thrifty.

**P** ST $5, LT $3.50.

# FLINT, Michigan
Bishop Intl Airport, 5 mi SW

🚗 $6, 15-20 min.

🚕 Avis, Dollar, Hertz.

# FLORENCE, Italy
Peretola Airport, 3.1 mi (5 km) NW

🚗 Lit2500 ($1.75), 15 min. If fare is fixed, no tip. Otherwise tip 5-10%.

🚕 Avis, Hertz.

# FORT-DE-FRANCE, Martinique
Lamentin Airport, 4.4 mi (7 km) ESE

🚗 F53 ($9.65), 10 min. Or take a collective taxi, identified with TC sign on roof, for F4.1 (75¢). To Pointe du Bout resorts, F136 ($25), 30 min; Leyritz Plantation, F261 ($47), 75 min; Ste-Anne, F241 ($44), 60 min. If driver accepts a pet he can charge F3 (55¢). Tip 10%. 40% surcharge 8 pm-6 am.

**Scenic alternative** Take cab from airport to ferry dock: F53 ($9.65). Catch ferry across bay: F9 ($1.65). Departures at 6:30, 8, 9, 10, 11 am; 12:15, 1:30, 3, 4, 5, 6, 7, 8, 11:15 pm; 12:10 am. 20-min ferry crossing to town, landing adjacent to Meridien, Bakoua Beach, other hotels. Half the price of a cab and great fun if you're traveling light.

🚕 Avis, Budget, Carib, Dollar, Europcar, Hertz, InterRent, Milleville.

**P** F109 ($19.20)/day.

# FRANKFORT, Kentucky See LEXINGTON/
FRANKFORT, Kentucky.

## FRANKFURT, West Germany
Frankfurt-Main Airport, 7 mi (12 km) S

🚗 DM25-30 ($15-18), 15-25 min to central points. Tip 5%.

🚆 Airport has its own modern rail station, reached by escalators. To Frankfurt, buy ticket DM3.40 ($1.80) from machine in Hall B, baggage claim. Note that passengers without tickets pay DM40 ($21) fine aboard. Trains every 10 min. 11-min ride to Frankfurt Hauptbahnhof. Very comfortable. Ample floorspace for bags. Direct rail connections from airport to Mainz, Russelsheim, Wiesbaden, and to Dusseldorf, Dortmund, Cologne, Amsterdam, Munich, Vienna, Basel, other destinations.

🚆 **Lufthansa Airport Express** It "flies" 4 times daily between Frankfurt and Dusseldorf airports with intermediate stops in Bonn, Cologne Central Stn, Cologne-Deutz, and Dusseldorf Central Stn. Only passengers with valid plane ticket may use this service. Luggage automatically transferred from plane to train. Check-in: basement level "Unterm Flughafen" Area B, Counter E-99. Departures times can be found in Lufthansa timetable. Frankfurt to Dusseldorf, 2 hrs 40 min.

🚗 AK Autovermeitung, Avis, Europcar, Eurorent, Hertz, InterRent, Schuldt/Autohansa, Sixt/Budget.

**P** DM16 ($8.50) first 7 days per day; thereafter DM5 ($2.65) per day.

## FREEPORT, Grand Bahama Island
Freeport Intl Airport, 2 mi (3.2 km) NW

🚗 $2.50. 5-10 min. Tip 10%.

🚗 Avis, National.

## FRESNO, California
Fresno Air Terminal, 7 mi NE

🚗 $12-13, 15 min.

🚌 No. 26 bus outside airport entrance every 30 min 6:42 am-6:15 pm. 50¢.

🚙 Avis, Hertz, National.

## FT. LAUDERDALE, Florida
Ft. Lauderdale-Hollywood Intl Airport, 4 mi S

🚗 To downtown business area $8, beach hotels $11, Galt Ocean Mile $15.

🚐 Yellow Airport Limousine, $8-10 downtown, $6-8 beach hotels.

🚙 Ajax, Alamo, American Intl, Avis, Budget, Dollar, Enterprise, General, Hertz, National, Payless, Snappy, Thrifty.

## FT. MYERS, Florida
Southwest Regional Airport, 10 mi SE

🚗 Midtown $17, 25 min. To Sanibel Island $24, by reservation: 813-472-4160.

🚐 Sun Lines to Ft. Myers $7.50 each, minimum two.

🚌 Express Bus to Naples, Marco at 9:30, 10:30, 11:30 am; 1, 2, 3, 4:30, 5:30, 8, 9, 11:30 pm. 6:30 pm run to Naples only. Naples $8, Marco $12.

🚙 Avis, Budget, Dollar, Hertz, National, Value.

## FT. WAYNE, Indiana
Baer Field, 9 mi SW

🚕 $14, 15-25 min.

🚗 Avis, Budget, Hertz, National.

## FT. WORTH, Texas See DALLAS-FT. WORTH, Texas.

## FUNCHAL, Madeira Islands
Funchal Airport, 14.5 mi (23 km) NE

🚕 Esc500 ($3.75). 35 min. Tip 10%.

🚐 Hotels Casino Park, Madeira Palace, Reids, Savoy, Sheraton operate courtesy vans.

🚗 Avis, Hertz, Rodavante.

**P** Free.

## GENEVA, Switzerland
Cointrin Airport, 2.5 mi (4 km) NW

🚕 SF25 ($15.90) to InterContinental Hotel. Metered, tip usually included. 10-15 min.

🚆 6-min rail link between air terminal and Cornavin RR Station in downtown Geneva. Departures about every 10 min 5:30 am-12:20 am. Buy ticket in advance: SF5 ($3.20) with 5 franc coin. Plenty of baggage space. Also from Cointrin Airport there are direct rail connections via Lausanne to Neuchatel, Delemont, and Basle in the north; Berne, Lucerne, Zurich, St. Gall in the east; Sion, Brigue, and northern Italy to the south. Luggage may be checked through on the new "Baggage Fly" service for SF9 ($5.70). Ask Swiss Natl Railroads agent.

🚌 TPG (Transports Publics Genevais) No. 10 every 5-15 min 5:47 am-12:09 am. To Bel-Air (city center) and Cornavin Station. Picks up on departure level.

**Ski season** Direct buses from airport to French ski resorts—see Thomas Cook European Timetable.

🚘 ANSA, Avis, Europcar, Hertz, InterRent.

**P** ST SF15 ($9.50), LT SF6 ($3.80), some free.

## GENOA, Italy
Cristoforo Colombo Airport, 4.5 mi (7 km) W

🚖 Lit3500 ($2.50), 20 min. Tip 5-10%.

🚘 Avis, Budget, Europcar, Hertz, InterRent, Maggiore.

**P** Lit10,000 ($7)/day.

## GEORGETOWN, Grand Cayman
Owen Roberts Airport, 1 mi (1.6 km) SE

🚖 CI$5, 5 min. Tip 15%.

🚘 Avis, Dollar, Hertz, National, Payless.

## GIBRALTAR, Gibraltar
Gibraltar/North Front Airport, 1/2 mi (0.5 km) N

🚖 £1.5 ($2.50) for 1-2 passengers; 25p (40¢) each addl. 5 min. Baggage 15p per piece. Surcharges weekends, after midnight. Tip 10-15%.

🚐 Tour operators' courtesy coach meets flights. 10 min.

🚌 No. 3/3B bus every 30 min 8:30 am-8:30 pm. Pay driver 20p (35¢). Baggage OK. Route: Winston Churchill Ave., Smith Dorrien Ave., Line Wall Rd., Convent, Southport Gates, Europa Rd., Loreto Convent, Royal Naval Hospital, Lighthouse.

🚘 A.M. Capurro/British Car, Bland/Avis, Budget, Europa, Sterling/Hertz, Tour Africa/Niza.

**P** £2 ($3.25)/day.

# GOTHENBURG, Sweden
Landvetter Airport, 15.5 mi (25 km) E

🚕 Skr100 ($15.50) to Central Station, 20 min. No charge first 25 kg of luggage. Any extra, Skr5 (80¢). Tip 10%.

🚐 SAS Audis to any location in city. Skr70 ($10.90), buy ticket at departure desk. Leaves from main door of intl terminal.

🚌 City Terminal bus from intl terminal 2-3 times hourly 6 am-11:21 pm M-F, 5:45 am-11:15 pm Sat-Sun. Pay Skr25 ($3.90) aboard bus. 30-35 min to Central Station. Good baggage space.

🚗 Avis, Budget, Europcar, Hertz, InterRent.

P ST Skr30 ($4.67), LT Skr115 ($17.90)/week.

# GRAND JUNCTION, Colorado
Walker Field, 6 mi NE

🚕 $7.40, 15-20 min.

🚗 Avis, Budget, Hertz, National, Payless, Thrifty.

# GRAND RAPIDS, Michigan
Kent County Intl Airport, 11 mi SE

🚕 $11 flat fare, 15 min to Amway, downtown. $6.50 each addl passenger. If no taxis at airport, use "Taxi" phone in shelter area outside terminal.

🚗 Avis, Budget, Hertz, National.

P ST $10, LT $2.50/day, $15/week.

# GREEN BAY, Wisconsin
Austin Straubel Field, 8.5 mi SW

🚕 $9-9.75, extra passengers 50¢ each. 12-15 min.

Avis, Budget, Hertz, National.

**P** ST $4, LT $3.25, weekly $17.50.

## GREENSBORO HIGH POINT WINSTON-SALEM, North Carolina
Greensboro Regional Airport, 9 mi W of Greensboro, 18 mi E of Winston-Salem, 12 mi NE of High Point

 $16, 10-20 min to Greensboro; $27, 25-30 min to Winston-Salem; $14, 20 min to High Point.

 Airport Limousine Service. To Greensboro, High Point hourly on the half hour 5:30 am-12:30 am daily. $9.50. To Winston-Salem, hourly on the hour 5 am-midnight. $12-15. AMEX, MC, Visa.

 Avis, Budget, Dollar, Hertz, National.

## GREENVILLE/SPARTANBURG, South Carolina
Greenville/Spartanburg Airport, 15 mi NE of Greenville, 13 mi SW of Spartanburg

 $15, 20 min to Greenville; $30, 30 min to Spartanburg. Extra passengers 25¢ each.

 Avis, Hertz.

## GUADALAJARA, Mexico
Aeropuerto Miguel Hidalgo, 10.5 mi (17 km) S

 $1-5, by zone, 10-25 min. Tip 15%.

 Chapala-Guadalajara bus picks up outside intl arrivals door, hourly. 25¢, 40 min. Baggage OK.

 Alal, Aries, Arrasa, Avis, Dollar, Hertz, Interrenta, National, Odin, Ohara, Quick, Rent-Ford.

**P** P4800 ($3.50)/day.

# GUANGZHOU, China
Baiyun Airport, 7.4 mi (12 km) N

🚗 Train station, Dong Fang Hotel, China Hotel (all in center city), RY3 (85¢), 10 min; White Swan Hotel, RY15 ($4.20), 40 min; Garden Hotel, RY10 ($2.80), 20 min. Tip 5-10%.

🚌 CAAC bus from airport to city ticket office every 20 min 6 am-11 pm. RY0.50 (14¢), 20 min.

🚘 Self-drive cars not available in China.


# GUERNSEY, Channel Islands
Guernsey La Villiaze Airport, 4 mi (6.5 km) WSW

🚗 £4 ($6.85), 15 min to St. Peter Port. Tip 10-15%.

🚌 Guernseybus No. C1 & C2 from the airport forecourt every 30 min 8 am-9:30 pm. 50p (80¢). 20 min. Baggage OK.

🚘 Avis, Harlequin Hire.

**P** £2 ($3.45)/day.


# GULFPORT/BILOXI, Mississippi
Gulfport Municipal Airport, 4 mi NE of Gulfport, 13 mi W of Biloxi

🚗 $9.50, 15 min to Gulfport; $20, 15-20 min to Biloxi. **To New Orleans Intl Airport** Coastliner van at 3:30, 5:30, 7:30, 9, 10:30 am; 12:30, 2, 3:30, 5:30 pm. To Slidell stopover, $18 OW, $30 RT. To N.O. Intl, $29 OW, $50 RT, 2-1/2 hr. Info & res (US) 800-647-3957.

🚘 Avis, Budget, Dollar, Hertz, National, Thrifty.

# HALIFAX, Nova Scotia
Halifax Intl Airport, 25 mi NE

🚗 C$27 ($22.15).

🚌 Nova Charters bus meets flights. C$8 ($6.55). Serves all major hotels. 40-50 min ride into city. AMEX, MC, VISA.

🚗 Avis, Budget, Hertz, Thrifty, Tilden.

# HAMBURG, West Germany
Hamburg-Fuhlsbuttel Airport, 5.5 mi (8.5 km) N

🚗 DM22 ($12), 25-30 min into city. Tip: round up fare to nearest mark or 50 pfennig.

🚌 Airport-City bus every 20 min 6:20 am-10:20 pm from arrival hall. Pay DM8 ($4.35) to driver. Stops at Holiday Inn, Hauptbahnhof Kirchenallee (main RR station), ZOB (central bus station). About 25 min.

🚌 No. 110 to Ohlsdorf in northern section of city, where one transfers to city trains and U-Bahn. Bus, DM3.70 ($2) including transfer. Good choice for travelers without baggage.

🚗 Autohansa, Auto-Sixt, Avis, Europcar, Hertz, InterRent.

**P** ST DM10-12 ($5.30-6.40), LT DM6 ($3.20).

# HAMILTON, Bermuda
Bermuda Air Terminal, 9 mi E

🚗 $12, 30 min. To Southampton area, $20. Baggage 25¢ each, maximum $4. Tip 15%. Fares to hotels and guest houses range from $5 to $24 depending on distance. (Bermuda dollar is on a par with US dollar.)

🚌 Bermuda Aviation Services coach on demand to

hotels, guest cottages. $6.50-$12.50, 15-50 min.

🚌 Public bus to Hamilton leaves from S side of main terminal every 15 min 6:45 am-11:45 pm. $2.50, 45 min. Small baggage OK.

🚙 None.

P Free.

## HANNOVER, West Germany
Langenhagen Airport, 8 mi (12.8 km) N

🚗 DM30 ($16), 25 min. For tip, round up to nearest mark.

🚌 No. 60 direct to air terminal at rear of Hauptbahnhof where there are cabs for easy transfer of baggage. Bus leaves every 30 min 6 am-10:30 pm. DM4.40 ($2.35). 25-min trip.

🚙 Autohansa, Avis, Europcar, Hertz, InterRent, Sixt (Budget).

## HARARE, Zimbabwe
Harare Intl Airport, 10 mi (16 km) SE

🚗 Z$16 ($2.40), 20 min. No tip required.

🚌 Air Zimbabwe coach departs hourly each direction between airport and city terminal 6 am-11 pm. Z$2 (30¢), 20 min. Ticket must be purchased in advance at airport.

🚙 Avis, Hertz.

## HARRISBURG, Pennsylvania
Harrisburg Intl Airport, 11 mi SE

🚗 $14-15, 10 min.

🚙 Avis, Budget, Dollar, Hertz.

# HARTFORD, Connecticut/SPRINGFIELD, Massachusetts

Bradley Intl Airport, 14 mi N of Hartford, 18 mi S of Springfield

🚗 Hartford $21 flat rate, 15-20 min. Springfield $26-30, Torrington $40-50, Putnam $60-70, Norwich $60-70, Meriden $30-40, New Haven $60-70, New London $70-80, Bridgeport, $80-90, Stamford, $110-120.

🚌 **To Hartford** Airport Taxi Co. hourly 4:45 am-11:20 pm. $5 to Hilton, Ramada, Sheraton, Holiday Inn, Summit. **To Springfield** Peter Pan bus at 7, 9:15, 11:15 am; 1:15, 3:15, 5:15, 6:50, 9 pm; also 10:15 pm ex Sat. $7, 30-40 min to bus terminal at Main & Liberty.

🚌 Take Employee Shuttle bus from second island opposite baggage claim to Employees' Parking lot. Then "N" bus downtown at 6:18, 6:58, 7:58, 9:22, 10:22, 11:22 am; 12:22, 1:22, 2:22, 3:05, 4:23, 5:27, 6:05 pm. $1.15.

🚗 Avis, Budget, Dollar, Hertz, National.

**P** ST $10, LT $6/$25 per week.

# HAVANA, Cuba

Jose Marti Airport, 14 mi S

🚗 $11-15 (US currency accepted), 25-30 min. Cabs available all times.

# HELSINKI, Finland

Helsinki Vantaa Airport, 12 mi (19 km) N

🚗 Fmk90 ($19), 25-40 min to city center. Surcharge for more than 2 passengers. No tip.

🚌 Finnair bus 2-4 times an hour 6:10 am-11:25 pm. Pay Fmk13 ($3) on bus. 25-40 min to Hotel Inter-

Continental, Central Railway Station, other stops on request.

🚌 No. 614 to Central Bus Station, No. 615 to Central Railway Station. Several stops along way. Baggage space but less than on limo. Pay Fmk10 ($2.30) aboard. Departures every 20 min from 5:25 am weekdays, 6:10 weekends, to 11:05 pm. Not A/C. 30-40 min ride.

🚗 Avis, Budget, Europcar/Carop, Hertz, InterRent.

P ST Fmk120 ($27), LT Fmk25 ($5.80).

## HERMOSILLO, Mexico
Hermosillo Airport, 3.7 mi (6 km) W

🚕 $7, 10-15 min.

🚗 Avis, Budget, Hertz.

## HILO, Hawaii
Gen. Lyman Field, 3 mi E

🚕 $6, 8 min. Baggage, 30¢ each. Bicycles, surfboards extra.

🚗 Alamo, Avis, Budget, Dollar, Hertz, National, Travelers.

P $6/day.

## HILTON HEAD ISLAND, South Carolina
Hilton Head Airport, 10 mi NE of Sea Pines Plantation

🚕 $12 flat, 20 min. If no cab at airport, call Yellow: 686-6666.

🚗 American Intl, Avis, Budget, Hertz, National.

## HOBART, Tasmania
Hobart Airport, 12.5 mi (20 km) E

🚕 A$18 ($14.40), 15-20 min. To Sandy Bay, A$18 ($14.40), 20-25 min; to Northern Suburbs, A$20 ($16), 25 min; to Howrah, A$14.50 ($11.60), 20 min. Tip not necessary.

🚐 Red-Line meets flights, departs from outside terminal. A$3.50 ($2.80), 20 min to city center, casino.

🚗 Avis, Budget, Hertz, Thrifty.

**P** A40¢ (30¢)/day.

# HONG KONG
Hong Kong Intl Airport, 3 mi (4.8 km) NE of Tsim Sha Tsui, Kowloon; 6 mi (9.7 km) N of central Hong Kong Island

🚕 To Tsim Sha Tsui, Kowloon, HK$20-25 ($2.60-3.20), 15-20 min. To central Hong Kong Island including Cross Harbour Tunnel fee, HK$52-55 ($6.70-7), 35-45 min. To Causeway Bay, Hong Kong Island including tunnel fee, HK$44-48 ($5.65-6.15), 25-35 min. Pay fare on meter in Hong Kong currency. Tip: Round up to next HK$.

🚐 A1 Airbus to Kowloon hotels: Ambassador, Empress, Grand, Holiday Inn Golden Mile, Hongkong, Hyatt Regency, Imperial, International, Kowloon, Miramar, New Astor, New World, Park, Peninsula, Ramada Inn Kowloon, Sheraton, Windsor, YMCA. HK$5 (65¢), 30 min. A2 Airbus to Central/Wanchai hotels: Furama, Mandarin Oriental, Victoria. HK$7 (90¢), 45 min. A3 Airbus to Causeway Bay hotels: Excelsior, Lee Gardens, Park Lane Radisson. HK$7 (90¢), 30 min. All buses operate 6:50 am-11 pm every 15 min.

🚗 Avis (Far East Rent-a-Car Ltd.).

**P** HK$276 ($35.30)/day.

# HONOLULU, Hawaii

Honolulu Intl Airport, 4.5 mi NW of financial district, 8 mi NW of Waikiki

🚕 $8-9 to business district, 10-15 min. $13-15 to Waikiki, 25-30 min.

🚐 Choice of van services to Waikiki hotels, downtown, other Oahu points. $5 to Waikiki. Waikiki Express, 942-2177. Airport Motorcoach, 926-4747.

🚌 No. 19 or No. 20 bus from ramp every 20-30 min 6:28 am-11:30 pm. 60¢ exact. Baggage must be small enough to place on lap or under seat. 20-25 min to business district, 40-50 min to Waikiki.

🚗 Alamo, American Intl, Avis, Budget, Dollar, Hertz, National, Thrifty.

# HOUSTON, Texas

Houston Intercontinental Airport, 22 mi N

🚕 $24 flat rate, 30-50 min. United Cab accepts AMEX card.

🚐 Airport Express every 30 min 6:50 am-1 am to Hyatt Regency downtown, Galleria, Post Oak terminal/Greenway Plaza. $7.70.

✈ Air Link Airways. $49 downtown. Service to other points. Info & Res: 713-975-8989.

**To Hobby Airport** Continental Express/Emerald Air at 9:30, 11 am; 1:30, 3, 4:55, 6:30, 8:05 pm. $15 seat in an ATR-42. 10-min flight time. Continental passengers making connection ride free.

🚗 Agency, Avis, Budget, Dollar, General, Hertz, Holiday Payless, National, Snappy, Thrifty

**P** ST $5, LT $3

# HOUSTON, Texas
William P. Hobby Airport, 9.5 mi SE

🚗 $12-14, 30 min. To Houston Intercontinental Airport, $31, 60-75 min in heavy traffic. United Cab Co. accepts AMEX card.

🚐 Hobby Airport Limousine to Hyatt Regency, downtown; South Main; Post Oak, near Galleria; Greenway Plaza. $6. Every 30 min 6 am-11:30 pm.

🚌 No. 50 Heights or Downtown bus, 60¢ exact. About every 20 min 4:17 am-12:12 am M-F. Every 30-35 min Sat-Sun-Hol. 50 min downtown.

**To Houston Intercontinental** Continental Express/ Emerald Air at 7:05, 10:10 am; 12:25, 2:05, 4, 5:35, 7:10 pm. $15 seat in an ATR-42. 10-min flight. Free to Continental passengers making connection.

🚗 Agency, Avis, Budget, Dollar, General, Hertz, National, Snappy, Thrifty.

**P** ST $20, LT $5.

# HUNTSVILLE/DECATUR, Alabama
Huntsville-Madison County Jetport, 11 mi SW of Huntsville

🚗 $14.50 to Huntsville, 15-20 min. Decatur, $25. Cabs do not wait at airport—must be called.

🚐 Airport Limousine Service 6:30 am to last flight. $11-12 per person to Huntsville addresses, $15-20 to Decatur.

🚗 Avis, Budget, Dollar, Hertz.

# HYDERABAD, India
Hyderabad Airport, 12 mi (19 km) NW

�');Rs20 ($1.40), 25 min, to city center, RR station. To Secunderabad RR station, Rs15 ($1.05), 20 min. To Hyderabad Bus Depot, Rs25 ($1.75), 35 min. Baggage Rs5 (35¢) each. Tip Rs2 (15¢).

🚗 Rental cars not available in India.

## INDIANAPOLIS, Indiana
Indianapolis Intl Airport, 8 mi SW

🚕 $11, 15 min downtown. $12.75 midtown; $18.45 East Side; $24.05 Ft. Benjamin Harrison. 50¢ each addl passenger.

🚐 Shuttlexpress van 7 am-11 pm. $7.25 one person, $5.90 two or more to same address. Serves downtown hotels. $15 to East Side, College Park. **To Lafayette, Purdue** Lafayette United Limo every 2 hrs 6:30 am-10:30 pm. Info: 317-497-3828. **To Noblesville, Anderson, Ball State, Muncie** ABC Coach Lines at 10:50 am, 5:25, 9 pm. Info: 800-228-0814 (Indiana only).

🚌 No. 9W bus from sign at outer roadway. Service every 30-60 min 5:03 am-11:24 pm M-F. Sat hourly 5:32 am-9:34 pm. Sun-Hol hourly 7:32 am-6:36 pm. $1.05.

🚗 Ace, Avis, Budget, Dollar, Hertz, National.

**P** ST $9, LT $2.50. Shuttle.

## INVERCARGILL, New Zealand
Invercargill Airport, 2 mi (3.2 km) W

🚕 NZ$8-9 ($5.30-6), 5 min. No tip. To Bluff, NZ$25 ($16.60), 30 min. Cabs do not wait at airport. Use free phone to call Blue Star Taxi.

🚌 H&H Travel Line meets flights. NZ$1.50 ($1), 10 min.

🚗 Avis, Bluff, Budget, Hertz.

# ISTANBUL, Turkey
Yesilkoy (Ataturk) Airport, 15 mi (24 km) SW

🚕 T17500 ($5), 30-50 min to Taksim Sq; T16000 ($4), 30 min to Aksaray. Small orange cabs, not A/C. Baggage T1500 (35¢). No tip.

🚌 HAVAS bus every 30 min 6 am-10 am; then hourly to 2 pm; then every 30 min to 11 pm. To Sishane, Aksaray 30-50 min. Pay fare T1700 (45¢) aboard bus. Comfortable.

🚌 No. 96 bus every 55 min 7 am-9 pm from outside terminal to Taksim Sq, making several stops en route. Buy ticket for T1280 (20¢) at kiosk. Ride can take from 30 min to an hour depending on traffic. Not A/C but otherwise comfortable ride for traveler with light baggage.

🚗 Avis, Budget, Europcar, Hertz, InterRent, Kontuar, Kayhan.

P Free.

# IZMIR, Turkey
Adnan Menderes Airport, 10 mi (16 km) S

🚕 T14500 ($3) flat rate for up to 3 persons. 20 min to city. Small cabs—Fiats, Renaults.

🚌 Airport Bus operated by Turkish Airlines serves passengers on all carriers. T1600 (40¢), 25 min to Efes Hotel.

🚗 American Intl, Avis, Hertz, InterRent.

# JACKSON, Mississippi
Jackson Municipal Airport, 10 mi E

🚕 $12, $1.50 each addl passenger. 20 min.

🚌 Airport Limousine Service 6 am-2 am. One passenger $10 to any downtown business address; two passengers $8 each.

🚗 Avis, Budget, Hertz, National.

## JACKSONVILLE, Florida
Jacksonville Intl Airport, 17 mi N

🚗 $19 plus tolls, addl riders $1 each. 20-60 min.

🚗 Avis, Budget, Hertz, National.

P ST $12, LT $4

## JAKARTA, Indonesia
Soekarno-Hatta Intl Airport, 16 mi (26 km) W

🚗 Rp17,000-20,000 ($10-12), 50-60 min to Borobudur, Hilton, Mandarin. Rp400 (25¢) per bag. A larger tip is expected if more than one person rides in cab but Rp1700 ($1) should be OK.

🚗 Avis, National.

## JERSEY, Channel Islands
Jersey Airport, 5.5 mi (9 km) WNW of St. Helier

🚗 £4.50 ($7.70) tip included, 15 min to town. To Gorey, £6.50 ($11.15), 30 min.

🚌 Jersey Motor Transport every 20 min 7 am-10 pm. Pay driver 75p ($1.20). Stops at Mermaid Hotel, Quennevais, St. Aubin, Grand Hotel, and Weighbridge Bus Station, St. Helier. 30 min to St. Helier.

🚗 Europcar, Hertz.

P LT4.80 ($8.20)/day.

## JOHANNESBURG, South Africa
Jan Smuts Airport, 14.5 mi (23 km) W

🚗 Rn34.50 ($13.80), 30 min. No tip.

🚌 To Johannesburg Rn5.50 ($2.20), Pretoria Rn6.50 ($2.60). Pay aboard. 21 departures daily 6:15 am-midnight.

🚘 Avis, Budget, Imperial.

## JUNEAU, Alaska
Juneau Intl Airport, 10 mi N

🚗 $10-12 to downtown hotels, 15 min. To Mendenhall Glacier Visitor Center, $6, 5 min; to Auke Bay Ferry Terminal, $7, 10 min. Addl riders $1 each.

🚐 Service after each flight. $5, 15 min. To Baranof, Breakwater, Westmarks, Shiefields, ferry terminals.

🚌 Capital Transit System departs approx hourly 7:30 am-11:30 pm M-Sat. Pay driver 75¢. 20 min. Limited baggage space.

🚘 Avis, Budget, Hertz, National, Payless, Rent-A-Wreck, Ugly Duckling.

**P** ST $9, LT $4.50.

## KAHULUI, Maui, Hawaii
Kahului Airport, 2 mi NE

🚗 $5, 10 min. To Lahaina, $35, 40-60 min; to Kihei, $20, 20-25 min.

🚘 Alamo, Avis, Budget, Dollar, Hertz, Payless, Rent-A-Wreck.

## KAILUA-KONA, Hawaii
Ke-Ahole Airport, 8 mi NW

🚌 To hotels: King Kamehameha $11; Kona Hilton $13; Kona Surf $20; Kona Village $13; Westin Mauna Kea Beach $35; Sheraton Royal $21.

🚗 Alamo, American Intl, Budget, Dollar, Hertz, National.

## KALAMAZOO, Michigan
Kalamazoo County Airport, 4 mi SE

🚕 Downtown, Upjohn, $6.40, 10 min. To Battle Creek, $30 flat rate, 30-40 min. Extra passengers 50¢ each.

🚗 Avis, Budget, Hertz, National.

**P** ST $12, LT $2.50. Parking lot closed 11:30 pm-5:30 am and 11 pm Sat-6 am Sun.

## KANSAS CITY, Missouri
Kansas City Intl Airport, 18 mi NW

🚕 $21.90 downtown, 25-40 min. $25-27 Crown Center, Country Club Plaza. $35-40 Overland Park. Cab fares are deregulated and vary from company to company—rates are from Yellow dispatcher. Best to confirm fare in advance with cab driver.

🚐 KCI Express every 30 min 5:45 am-midnight. 25-40 min to downtown hotels. $9 OW, $17 RT. To Crown Center, Plaza, $10 OW, $19 RT. To Johnson County hotels, 8:15 am-10:15 pm hourly. $14 OW. MC, VISA accepted. Leaves from Terminal C, Gate 63 (take airport shuttle if that's too long a walk).

🚌 No. 29 KCI airport bus from Terminal A at 6:54, 7:16, 7:45 am; 2:54, 4:52 pm. Also picks up at terminals B, C. 90¢ fare. 55 min to downtown KC, 65 min to Plaza. No special baggage space. To catch this bus you must go down ramp at end of terminal to outer circle roadway and stand at airport employees' shelter.

🚕 Alamo, Avis, Budget, Dollar, Hertz, National, Payless, Snappy, Thrifty.

**P** ST $10, LT $2.50-5. Shuttle.

## KAUAI, Hawaii
Lihue Airport, 2 mi E of Lihue

🚐 To Coco Palms Resort, $15; Sheraton Princeville, $55; Kapaa, $18; Lihue Convention Center, $5. Cabs are expensive in Kauai. Tourists staying more than a couple of days will do better renting a car, locals advise.

🚕 Alamo, Avis, Budget, Dollar, Hertz, National, Tropical.

## KEY WEST, Florida
Key West Intl Airport, 1 mi SE

🚐 $4 flat rate, 10 min to Duvall St.

🚕 Avis, Budget, Dollar, Hertz, Thrifty, Value.

## KINGSTON, Jamaica
Norman Manley Intl Airport, 11 mi SE

🚐 J$70 ($13.35), 40 min.

🚕 American Intl, Avis, Budget, Dollar, Hertz, National.

## KNOXVILLE, Tennessee
Knoxville Airport, 12 mi S

🚐 $14 for 1-2 passengers, $7 each 3 or more. 25-30 min.

🚌 Airport Limousine leaves 10 min after each flight arrives. $10 OW, $17 RT to downtown hotels.

🚕 Avis, Budget, Dollar, Hertz, National.

## KRALENDIJK, Bonaire
Flamingo Airport, 2 mi (3.5 km) S

🚕 NAfl9 ($5), 5 min. To Flamingo Beach Hotel, NAfl7.20 ($4); Bonaire Beach Hotel;NAfl14 ($8); Habitat, NAfl15 ($8.50); Entrejol, NAfl14 ($8); Oil Terminal, NAfl35 ($20); Playa Grandi, NAfl35 ($20); Punta Blancu, NAf17.5 ($10); Rode Pan, NAfl26.25 ($15); Zuidkust (AISCO), NAfl21 ($12); Rincon, NAf26.10 ($14.50); Sand Dollar Beach Club, NAf14.40 ($8). Surcharges: 8 pm-midnight, 25%; midnight-6 am, 50%. More than 4 passengers, 20% each addl. Tip 10%.

🚗 AB Carrental, Avis, Boncar/Budget, Evertsz, Sunray, Total Carrental.

P Free.

## KUALA LUMPUR, Malaysia
Subang Intl Airport, 14 mi (22.5 km) SW

🚕 RGT22 ($8.80), 30-40 min. Check posted rates. Buy coupon at booth, give to driver. Tip optional. 50% surcharge midnight-8 am.

🚐 Comfortable A/C coach, RGT5-10 ($2-4), 30 min.

🚗 Avis, Europcar, Hertz, Sintat.

## LA PAZ, Mexico
General Marquez de Leon Airport, 7 mi (11.3 km) N

🚕 $7, 15 min.

🚗 Avis, Budget, Hertz.

## LAHORE, Pakistan
Lahore Airport, 2 mi (3.2 km) NW

🚌 Hilton Intl, Pearl Continental provide free airport service.

🚗 Avis.

## LAKE TAHOE, California
Lake Tahoe Airport, 5 mi S

🚕 To Casino Core, $9.50-12, 20-30 min.

🚌 Showboat, Dial-A-Ride coaches meet flights. $3, 15-20 min to Harrah's, Harvey's, High Sierra, Caesar's, etc. Purchase tickets in advance in terminal. **To Reno Intl Airport from casinos** LTR service, $12, 90 min.

🚗 Avis, Budget, Hertz.

**P** $3/day; $50/month.

## LANSING, Michigan
Capital City Airport, 4 mi NW

🚕 $7 downtown, 10 min.

🚌 Yellow Cab operates van downtown. $3.50 per person. Meets most flights— use white courtesy phone to call.

🚗 Avis, Budget, Hertz, National.

## LARNACA, Cyprus
Larnaca Intl Airport, 4 mi (6.4 km) S of Larnaca, 33 mi (53 km) SE of Nicosia

🚕 To center of town Cy£1.50 ($3). Shared taxis serve entire island from Larnaca.

🚗 Avis, Budget, Fivos, Hertz, InterRent, A. Petsas & Sons, Thames.

## LAS VEGAS, Nevada
McCarran Intl Airport, 7 mi S

🚕 $11 to The Strip, $17 downtown.

🚌 Gray Line Airport Express. To The Strip, $3 OW, $5.25 RT. To Downtown, $4.25 OW, $7 RT. Departures every 20 min 5 am-2 am. Stops at all major hotels. For return from hotels, call 702-384-1234.

🚗 Ajax, Alamo, American Intl, Avis, Budget, Dollar, Enterprise, General, Hertz, National, Payless, Snappy, Thrifty.

## LENINGRAD, USSR
Leningrad Pulkovo Airport, 10.5 mi (17 km) S

🚕 Rs5-7 ($1.50-2 at official exchange rate), 15-20 min. Tip: Rs1.

🚌 Aeroflot service to office on Nevsky Prospekt.

🚆 Express bus links airport and Pobyedi station of Metro. 20-min run. Metro fare 5 kopecks (1¢) through turnstile. Nevsky Prospekt, center city, is sixth stop. Total travel time 40-60 min including connections. Cabs available on street. **Note:** Although most Westerners rely on Intourist to make all travel arrangements in the Soviet Union, it is quite possible to do so oneself in the major cities. Traveling unescorted on the Metro is a superb introduction to everyday life. Ask Intourist for English language maps; carry kopecks for fares.

🚗 Intourist makes arrangements.

## LEXINGTON/FRANKFORT, Kentucky
Blue Grass Field, 6 mi W of Lexington

🚕 $9, 15 min to Lexington; $39, 40 min to Frankfort.

🚗 American Intl, Avis, Budget, Dollar, Hertz, Snappy, Thrifty.

## LIMA, Peru
Jorge Chavez Intl Airport, 5 mi (8 km) W

🚕 About $11 downtown, no extras, no tip. Agree on price before getting in cab. 30-45 min. Colectivos—shared-ride cabs—charge about half of regular cab price, operate from 6 am-6 pm. Stop at La Colmena 73, midway between Gran Bolivar and Crillon hotels.

🚌 Trans Hotel bus every 20 min. $5. Stops at hotels and other places on request. Also inquire about hotel vans.

🚌 Airport Bus at Enatru station outside airport. Hourly, $1.50, baggage space. Terminus at Ave. La Colmena. Long ride—90+ min.

🚗 Avis, Budget, National, Hertz.

## LINCOLN, Nebraska
Lincoln Municipal Airport, 5 mi NW

🚕 $6.50, 10-15 min.

🚗 Avis, Budget, Hertz, National.

## LISBON, Portugal
Lisboa (Portela) Airport, 4.5 mi (7 km) N

🚕 Esc400 ($2.60), 15-20 min to Ritz. Taxi rank at left outside arrival hall. For several bags driver can charge 50% more than meter. Tip 10%.

🚌 Green Line bus every 15 min 7:30 am-9:20 pm M-Sat, every 20 min Sun. Pay driver Esc170 ($1.10). 35-40 min to Santa Apolonia RR station by river in old Alfama section. Little baggage room. Bus connects with subway at Entrecampos.

🚗 Avis, Budget, Europcar, Guerin, Hertz/Renorte, InterRent/Global Rent, Travelcar, Turincar.

**P** ST Esc1900 ($12.50), LT/6 months Esc5050 ($33).

## LITTLE ROCK, Arkansas
Little Rock Regional Airport (Adams Field), 3.5 mi SE

🚕 $7.50, each addl rider $1. 10-15 min.

🚌 **To Hot Springs** Collins Airport Service about every 2 hrs 8:30 am-11 pm. $15 per person.

🚗 Avis, Dollar, Hertz, National.

## LONDON, England
Gatwick Airport, 27 mi (43 km) S

🚕 £40-45 ($68-77) to central London. Tip 10-15%. 40-90 min trip depending on time of day.

🚌 No. 777 bus every 30 min 6:20 am-6 pm, then hourly to 10 pm. Departs Gatwick South Terminal. £3.50 ($6). 70 min to Victoria Coach Station.

🚆 Gatwick Express every 15 min 6:05 am-10:50 pm; then every 30 min to 12:05 am; then hourly to 6:05 am. Fares: £5 ($7.50) 2nd Class, £7.50 ($12.85) 1st Class. Wide doors, automatic inside doors, ample baggage space. 30 min express ride to Victoria Station. No service Christmas Day. **To Heathrow Airport** Speedlink every 30 min 6:20 am-9:20 pm, then hourly to 12:20 am, then 2:20 am. Fare £6 ($10.25); midnight-5 am, £12 ($20.50). 60-min ride to Heathrow. No service Christmas Day.

🚗 Avis, Budget, Europcar, Hertz.

**P** ST £6.80 ($11.65) first 5 days, £2.80 ($4.80) each addl day. LT £5.60 ($9.60) first 2 days, £2.80 ($4.80) each addl day.

## LONDON, England
Heathrow Airport, 15 mi (25 km) W

🚗 To Central London £22 ($37.60), 30-50 min. Addl passengers 20p (35¢) each, bags 10p each. Surcharge late evening, Sat, Sun, Hol 60p ($1). After 8 pm Dec. 24 to 6 am Dec. 26, £2 ($3.50) surcharge. Tip porter 40p per bag; tip driver 10-15%. Traditional black cabs, also red and green. Cab sharing available in cabs so marked. Fare each passenger pays as percentage of full fare: two, 65%; three, 55%; four, 45%; five, 40%.

🚌 Flightline 767 bus from each terminal and Central Bus Station to Victoria Coach Station every 30 min 5:45 am-6:15 pm, then hourly to 9:15 pm. Fare £3.50 ($6) OW, £5 ($8.50) RT, 65 min. Driver loads baggage, very comfortable ride, onboard WC.

🚆 Heathrow terminals are stations on Piccadilly Line. Moving walkways to station—baggage carts can be taken to entrance. Buy ticket at counter or from machine, £1.70 ($3) to Piccadilly. Comfortable for travelers with small baggage. Trains every 3 min peak times, every 7 min off-peak & Sun, from 5:08 am-11:49 pm Mon-Sat, 6:01 am-10:27 pm Sun. No service Christmas Day. 47-min average to Piccadilly, 55 min to King's Cross, 61 min to Liverpool St. Note there may be stairs to climb at some exits.

🚌 Airbus A1 to Victoria BR Stn every 20-30 min 6:20 am-10:20 pm. A2 to Euston Railway Station every 20-30 min 6:10 am-9:05 pm. 50-60 min ride. Fare £4 ($6.85).

US, Canadian, French, German currency accepted. Ample baggage space, comfortable ride. These magnificent red double-deckers are a sightseer's delight and fast. They stop at major hotel areas en route. **To Gatwick Airport** Speedlink 747 from terminals and Central Bus Station every 30 min 4:30 am-9:30 pm, then 10:30 pm, 12:40 am. Fare £6 ($10.25). Midnight to 4:59 am, £12 ($20.50). 60 min to Gatwick terminal. No service Christmas day.

🚗 Avis, Budget, Europcar, Hertz.

**P** ST £26 ($44.50); LT £4.50 ($7.70) per day through 5 days, £4.25 ($7.30) per day from day 6. **Bus connections elsewhere** Many bus routes connect Heathrow with the surrounding countryside. Inquire at Central Bus Station.


# LONDON, ENGLAND
London City Airport, 6 mi E

🚗 £8 ($13.70), 25 min to the City. Advise airplane cabin crew during flight and a taxi can be ordered in advance of landing.

🚆 Short walk to Silvertown Station on British Rail's North London Link. Fare £2 ($3.40). Connects to Underground District Line at West Ham, to Central Line at Stratford.

**River Bus** Free shuttle from terminal to high speed catamaran on the Thames. Service hourly 7:30 am-6:30 pm M-F except holidays. £5 ($8.50). 30-min ride to Charing Cross Pier, near Embankment station of Underground.

🚗 Europcar, Hertz.

**P** ST £22 ($37.60), LT £5 ($8.50) first day, £3 ($5) each addl day.

# LONDON, England

Stansted Airport, 37 mi (59 km) NE of London, 4 mi (6.4 km) NE of Bishop's Stortford

🚕 Aircars Taxi Service has a counter in arrivals hall. £4 ($6.85), 10-15 min to British Rail Station in Bishop's Stortford, where there is service to Liverpool Street Station, London, a 45-50 min ride, for £4.50 ($7.70) standard class. Service about twice an hour, more at peak times. Hourly Sundays.

🚆 Nos. 333, X70, 370, 33 operate between airport and Bishop's Stortford Station. Service about every 30 min. 90p ($1.50). 15-min ride.

**To Heathrow, Gatwick** Premier Travel coach every 2 hrs 4:20 am-6:20 pm. 80 min to Heathrow, 1 hr 40 min to Gatwick.

🚗 Budget, Europcar/National/Tilden.

**P** ST £1 ($1.70) first day, £5 ($8.50) each day thereafter. LT £1 ($1.70).

# LONG BEACH, California

Long Beach Municipal Airport, 24 mi SE of Los Angeles

🚕 To Hyatt Regency, Queen Mary area of Long Beach, $16, 20 min. To LAX, $35, 40-50 min; to downtown LA, $40-45, 40-70 min.

🚐 **To Long Beach Harbor** SuperShuttle $20 first passenger, $7 each addl. **To Disneyland** SuperShuttle $33 first passenger, $7 each addl. **Anaheim (Disneyland) & Orange County destinations** Luxe Livery/Airport Transportation. Fares range $21-33. Advance reservations: (US) 800-854-8171. From Long Beach upon arrival 800-422-4267. Long Beach-Disneyland fare $23 first person, $7 each addl to same dropoff. AMEX, MC, VISA.

🚌 **To LA** No. 457 RTD Express Bus M-F am only from Airport Park-Ride lot at 6:00, 6:13, 6:31, 6:49, 7:07, 7:25, 7:45, 8:05 am. $2.70, bills OK. Hour ride to 5th & Flower, downtown. Room for small baggage. Catch express return from 6th & Flower pm. Ask driver for schedule. **To Long Beach** No. 111 Broadway/Lakewood bus every 30 min 6:21 am-12:11 am M-F; hourly 7:05 am-11:50 pm Sat-Sun-Hol.

🚐 **To LAX** SuperShuttle $20 first psgr, $6 each addl. Reserve a day in advance: 213-338-1111. AMEX, MC, VISA. Also Airport Coach at 10:25 a.m. 30 min to Terminal 1. $8. **To Orange County, Ontario Intl airports** Airport Coach: 800-772-5299, 714-457-1992.

🚗 Avis, Budget, Dollar, Hertz, National.

**P** ST $12; LT $6, $30/week.

## LOS ANGELES, California
Los Angeles Intl Airport, 15 mi SW

**INFO, SCHEDULES** Inquire at "Ground Transport" booth outside each terminal. Airport info by phone: 213-646-5252.

🚗 Downtown LA $26.50, 30-35 min. Anaheim/Disneyland, $85. Long Beach Airport/downtown, $46-50. Century City $24-26. Fares include $2.50 airport tax.

🚐 **Door-to-door vans on demand** To hotels, offices, and residences throughout Los Angeles and Orange counties. Among 24 or more operators, SuperShuttle is largest and serves widest territory. Collect bags, call 417-8988 to reach dispatcher. Wait at "Taxi" sign on island outside lower level. Typical hotel fares: downtown LA, Anaheim/Disneyland $10; Century City $8; Irvine $16.

Typical residence, business fares: Burbank $27; Hermosa Beach $8; Irvine $37; Santa Monica $12; Van Nuys South $27. Reservation required 3 hrs in advance for return trip. Res/info: 800-554-6458. AMEX, MC, VISA. Rideshare vans offer convenience compared to scheduled bus, cost saving compared to taxi in many cases. But trade-off is time waiting for van to arrive and further delay if driver circles for other fares or drops you off last.

🚌 All public buses to downtown and elsewhere board at RTD City Bus Center, just outside airport. Free shuttle bus "C" every 10 min 24 hrs a day. A/C, clean, baggage racks. 7-min ride to transfer point. **Downtown LA** No. 439 Express Mon-Fri from Bay 11 at 6:11, 6:46, 7:27, 8:07, 8:47 am, then 37 min past the hour to 2:37, then 3:10, 3:38, 4:23, 5:08, 5:53, 6:37 pm. Fare $1.50. 44 min to Flower & 7th, downtown. No. 42 operates at other times from Bay 13. Fare $1.10. **Other destinations** RTD buses also serve West Hollywood, Marineland, Long Beach, Redondo Beach, Whitwood Center, Lynwood, UCLA Van Nuys-Lakeview Terrace, Pico & Westwood, UCLA via Brentwood, Ramada Inn Norwalk, UCLA via Sepulveda, West Imperial Terminal. Info: 213-626-4455.

**Interairport Connections** To Burbank, Long Beach, John Wayne & Ontario airports. SuperShuttle: call 417-8988 from LAX; elsewhere, toll-free 800-554-6458. **To Ontario Intl Airport** Airportcoach at 9 am; 1:15, 7, 9:45 pm. $12. 90-min. Service continues to Palm Desert, $20. Info: 714-491-3500.

🚗 Avis, Budget, Dollar, Hertz, National.

**P** ST $10; LT $3-4, first 2 hrs free. Free shuttle buses "B" and "C" to long-term lots every 10 min 24 hrs a day.

## SCHEDULED SERVICE TO & FROM OTHER POINTS

**Van Nuys & San Fernando Valley** FlyAway bus from each terminal every 30 min 5:30 am-midnight. Then 12:15, 12:30, 1:15, 2:15, 2:45, 3:30, 4:15, 4:45 am. $4.50 OW, $8 RT. Service to Van Nuys Airport Bus Terminal (7610 Woodley, corner of Saticoy). Parking at Van Nuys available for $1/day up to 30 days max. Info: 818-994-5554. **Lancaster, Palmdale, Newhall** Antelope Valley Airport Express. 8 departures between 7:30 am and 10 pm. Newhall $12, Lancaster/Palmdale $25. Info & res: 805-945-2LAX. **Ventura, Oxnard, Camarillo, Thousand Oaks, Westlake Village, Woodland Hills** Great American Stage Line every 75-90 min 7 am-11 pm. Info: 805-375-1361. **Santa Barbara** Santa Barbara Airbus every 1-1/2 - 2 hrs 7:30 am-11 pm. $26 OW, $48 RT. 2-1/2 hr trip. Also serves Carpinteria, Montecito, Goleta, Isla Vista. Res: 800-423-1618 (Cal) **Bakersfield** Airport Bus of Bakersfield at 7:30, 10:30 am; 2:30, 6:30, 10:30 pm. 2-1/2-hr trip. $25. **San Bernardino, Riverside, Palm Springs, Palm Desert** Airportcoach at 9 am, 1:15, 7, 9:45 pm. $12-20. Info: 714-491-3500.

🚁 L.A. Helicopter hourly connections to Burbank, City of Commerce, City of Industry, Long Beach Airport. Heliport atop parking lot opposite Terminal 4. Info & res: 213-642-6600.

# LOUISVILLE, Kentucky
Standiford Field, 5 mi S

🚗 $10 flat, addl riders 30¢ each, 15-20 min.

🚌 Airport Limousine hourly 9:10 am-6:10 pm, $4.50. Meets flights other times. No Sat service. Sun hourly 3:30-9:30 pm. Stops at Galt House, Seelbach, Hyatt.

🚌 No. 2 Second St. bus at 6, 7:16, 8:03, 9:55, 11:24 am; 12:57, 2:02, 2:57, 3:36, 4:43, 5:06, 6:28, 8:44, 10:51 pm M-F. 35 min to 1st & Market downtown. 60¢.

🚗 Agency, Avis, Budget, Dollar, Hertz, National, Snappy, Thrifty.

## LUBBOCK, Texas
Lubbock Intl Airport, 6 mi N

🚕 $9.50, $2 each addl rider. 12 min.

🚗 Avis, Budget, Dollar, Hertz, National.

## LUXEMBOURG City
Findel Airport, 3.75 mi (6 km) E

🚕 LF500-600 ($12.60-15.10), 15-20 min to Central RR Station. For more than one bag LF20 (50¢) each extra.

🚐 Luxair bus every 30 min 6:05 am-10:40 pm. 15-20 min to Air Terminus Luxair near Central Station. Pay LF120 ($3) aboard. Not A/C.

**Icelandic passengers** May use free motorcoach transfer to principal points in Belgium, Holland, W. Germany. Info, reservations: 800-223-5500. **Luxavia passengers from Johannesburg** Similar service into W. Germany.

🚌 Luxembourg Ville every 30 min from main terminal. Stops at Youth Hostel, City Center, Central Station. Pay LF25 (60¢) aboard. No special place for baggage but comfortable ride of 15-20 min.

🚗 Avis, Budget, Continental/Lux, Europcar, Hertz, InterRent.

**P** ST LF200 ($5), LT LF100 ($2.50).

## LYONS, France

Lyon/Satolas Airport, 15.5 mi (25 km) E of Lyons; 65 mi (105 km) NW of Grenoble; 75 mi (122 km) SW of Geneva, Switzerland

🚖 F140 ($22), 20 min; night fare, F200 ($31.30). To Grenoble, F550 ($86), 60 min.

🚌 Aeroport Intl coach departs every 20-30 min 6 am-11 pm. Pay driver F36 ($5.65). 45-min ride stopping at Gare de la Part-Dieu, Perrache Station, Jean Mace, Nouvelles Galeries, Mairie du 8e.

Coach service also available to Grenoble, Annecy, Aix-les-Bains, Chambery. Inquire at airport information desk.

🚗 Avis, Citer, Europcar, Hertz, InterRent, Mattei, Milleville-Budget.

**P** ST F23 ($3.60), LT F20 ($3.15).

## MADISON, Wisconsin

Dane County Regional Airport, 5 mi NE

🚖 $7.20, 12 min to Capitol; $8-10, 12-15 min to University area.

🚌 Airport Limousine meets flights: $5 to Capitol, $6 to University.

🚗 Avis, Dollar, Hertz, National.

**P** ST $9, LT $3.

## MADRID, Spain

Barajas Airport, 7.5 mi (12 km) NE

🚖 Pta1330-1662 ($10-13) to Plaza Colon, 30 min. Extras: Pta50 (40¢) nights, Hol, Pta50 (40¢) each bag. Make certain meter is at zero upon entering cab. Tip 10%.

🚌 Airport Bus outside arrival terminal. Pta210 ($1.75), pay upon boarding. Every 30 min 4:45 am-1:51 am. Comfortable ride, plenty of baggage space. A/C. Stops at Avenida America, Francisco Silvela, Maria de Molina, Velazquez, Serrano, Ortega y Gasset, Plaza Colon.

🚗 Avis, Europcar, Hertz, InterRent/Atesa.

**P** Pta330 ($2.60)/day.

## MANCHESTER, England
Manchester Airport, 10 mi (16 km) S

🚕 £9-12 ($15.40-20.50) to central Manchester, 20-35 min. For journeys outside city, determine fare in advance with driver.

🚌 Airport Express 757 from Airport Bus Stn adjacent to Intl Arrivals hall. Stops at National Coach Stn, Piccadilly Bus Stn, Victoria Rail Stn. Every 30 min 5:20 am-7:20 pm, every 45 min 8:05 pm-11:05 pm Mon-Sat. 45-60 min service Sun. Pay £1.40 ($2.40) to driver. 40-45 min.

🚗 Avis, Europcar, Hertz.

**P** ST £5 ($8.50), LT £2.40 ($4.10).

## MANCHESTER, New Hampshire
Manchester Airport, 5 mi SE

🚕 $9, 50¢ each addl rider. 15 min.

🚗 Avis, Budget, Hertz.

## MANILA, Philippines
Ninoy Aquino Intl Airport, 5 mi (8 km) S

🚕 R&E, MIATDA taxis, yellow colored, A/C, metered. PP37.50 ($1.80), 15 min to city center. Non A/C charge less. Pay in pesos, tip optional.

🚌 Metro Manila Transit Love Bus every 5 min 6 am-6 pm M-Sat. Pay fare PP7 (35¢) before boarding. 20-60 min to Santa Cruz, Cubao, depending on traffic. Tends to be crowded, not much room for bags.

🚗 Avis, Hertz, National.

**P** PP49 ($2.30)/day.

## MARSEILLES, France
Aeroport Marseilles Provence, 17 mi (28 km) NW

🚗 F150 ($24.50) daytime, F230 ($37.50) night. 30 min to city. Baggage F5 (80¢) each. Tip 10%.

🚐 Aeroport Marseille Provence bus to and from Gare St. Charles every 20 min 6:10 am-9:50 pm. A 30-min trip. Fare F32 ($5.25). Service also to Aix-en-Provence, F25.50 ($4.15), 35 min.

🚗 Avis, Budget, Citer, Europcar, Hertz/Mattei, InterRent.

**P** ST F36 ($5.90), LT F16 ($2.60).

## MARTHA'S VINEYARD, Massachusetts
Dukes County Airport, 5 mi W of Edgartown, 5 mi S of Vineyard Haven

🚗 Hathaway Taxi: $10 flat rate for 2, $1 each addl, 15 min.

🚗 Hertz, National.

## MATAMOROS, Mexico
Servando Canales Airport, 10 mi (16 km) S

🚗 $6, 25 min.

🚗 Avis, Budget, Dollar.

## MAZATLAN, Mexico
Rafael Buelna Intl Airport, 14 mi (23 km) SW

🚗 $10, 25 min.

🚕 Budget, Avis.


## MELBOURNE, Australia
Melbourne Intl Airport, 15 mi (24 km) NW

🚗 A$14-15 ($9.80-10.50), 20-35 min to Regent Hotel, Bourke Street area. No tip.

🚌 Skybus every 30-60 min 6:30 am-11:30 pm, A$6 ($4.20). Terminus is Skybus Travel Center, 58 Franklin St.

🚕 Avis, Budget, Hertz, Thrifty.

**P** ST A$10 ($7), LT A$4.50 ($3.15).


## MEMPHIS, Tennessee
Memphis Intl Airport, 9 mi SE

🚗 $13, 20 min to Peabody, downtown. St. Jude Hospital $13, Germantown $16, NAS Memphis/Millington $32.50, Olive Branch $23, Southaven $13, West Memphis $25.

🚌 Airport Limousine Service, $6. Use limo phone if none is waiting.

🚌 No. 32 bus at sign, lower level. Every 20-50 min 6:47 am-6:16 pm M-Sat. No Sun. 85¢ plus 10¢ transfer. Change at Fairgrounds to No. 56 or No. 10. Total time to 2nd & Madison downtown, 75-80 min.

🚕 Avis, Budget, Hertz, National.

**P** ST $10, LT $3.

# MERIDA, Mexico
Manuel Crescencio Rejon Airport, 5 mi (3 km) SW

🚗 $6, 15 min.

🚕 Avis, Hertz, Volkswagen.

# MEXICO CITY, Mexico
Benito Juarez Airport, 6.2 mi (10 km) E of Zona Rosa

🚗 Buy trip ticket at Authorized Taxi Service booth. Fare to Zona Rosa about $4 in airport cab, white and mustard colored. Four ride for price of one. Ride time 30 min. Tip not necessary but won't be refused. Sign in arrivals area cautions "Use only authorized service. The use of any other service is on your own responsibility," meaning it may cost double.

🚆 Luggage not allowed on Metro though a large brief-case, small shoulder bag probably OK. Metro is clean, fast, modern, cheap. Good way around in nonrush hours. Entrance marked by M on pylon to left outside terminal, a 3-4 min walk around parking garage. Fare P200 (9¢).Airport Station is on Line 5. To Zona Rosa take Pantitlan train. At Pantitlan (one stop), change to Observatorio train on Line 1. Get off at Insurgentes, in Zona Rosa.

🚕 Avis, Budget, Dollar, Hertz, National.

**P** ST $6.75, LT $4.95.

# MIAMI, Florida
Miami Intl Airport, 7 mi NW

🚗 $13, 20 min. Miami Beach $18-28, Key Biscayne $22, cruise ships $12, Doral Country Club, $13, Ft. Lauderdale-Hollywood Intl Airport $35. Flat fares to hotels in airport region range $4.50-7.

🚐 Red Top meets flights. $6.75, 15-30 min to downtown hotels. Miami Beach $8, cruise ships $5.50, Key Biscayne $10.25, Doral CC $6.75, Ft. Lauderdale-Hollywood Intl Airport $11.50, Boca Raton $19.50, Hallandale/Miramar $11.50.

🚌 No. 7 Metro bus to NW 2nd Ave. & 5th St. downtown. M-F 5:27 am-9:07 pm, 35-40 min downtown. **$1** exact fare. To ride Metrorail, take transfer for 25¢. Hourly service Sat-Sun 6:25 am-5:16 pm. **To Miami Beach** No. J Metro bus every 20-30 min 4:39 am-11:31 pm; hourly Sun 5:40 am-8:40 pm. On Miami Beach, follows Collins Ave. route from 39th to 72nd St. $1.

🚗 Alamo, American Intl, Avis, Budget, Dollar, General, Hertz, Inter American, Lindo's, National, Thrifty, U.S.A., Value.

**P** ST $15, LT $6.

**To Key West** Greyhound at 7:25 am, 12:40, 6:20 pm. Intermediate stops at Coral Gables, Homestead, Key Largo, Isla Morada, Layton, Marathon, Tavernier, Perrine, Big Pine Key. Info: 305-374-7222.

## MIDLAND, Texas
Midland Regional Airport, 10 mi W

🚕 To Midland $12, 15-20 min. Fare slightly less to Odessa. Addl riders 25¢ each.

🚗 Avis, Budget, Dollar, Hertz, National.

## MILAN, Italy
Forlanini-Linate Airport, 4.5 mi (7 km) E

🚕 Lit15,000 ($11.25), 15-20 min. Take yellow cab with meter, not a gypsy. Tip included in fare but bags are Lit250 addl each.

🚌 SEAV coach to Milano Centrale, largest railway terminal in the world. 7 am-11 pm at 20-30 min intervals. Look for orange SEAV sign at national arrivals exit. Fare Lit1700 ($1.30) purchased in advance at train station or from driver at airport. Luggage space beneath bus. 23-min ride. Bus also goes to Garibaldi Station.

🚌 ATM No. 73—look for sign and bus shelter near SEAV. Every 12-23 min 6 am-12:50 pm. Fare Lit500 (40¢). Buy ticket from machine at bus stop. Bus terminates at Piazza San Babila near Duomo with connection to Milano Metro. No baggage space, likely to be crowded.

🚗 Avis, Budget, Europcar, Hertz, InterRent/Autotravel, Italy by Car, Maggiore, Tirreno.

P Lit13,000 ($9.75).

## MILAN, Italy
Milano/Malpensa Intl Airport, 28 mi (45 km) NW

🚗 Lit60,000 ($45), 60 min.

🚌 Airpullman meets intl flights between 8 am and midnight. 60-min ride. Stops at Centrale, Garibaldi stations in Milan.

🚌 Bus to Gallarate RR Station then rail to Milan, Porta Garibaldi Station. Service approx hourly 6:10 am-6:50 pm. Total journey time 65-100 min.

🚗 Avis, Budget, Europcar, Eurotrans, Hertz, InterRent/Autotravel, Maggiore.

P Lit13,000 ($9.75).

## MILWAUKEE, Wisconsin
General Mitchell Intl Airport, 7 mi S

🚗 $14-16, 15-25 min downtown. Bayside, $28-31;

Menomonee Falls, $31-37; Brookfield, $22-28; New Berlin, $17-22; Muskego, $20-25. Addl passengers 25¢ ea.

🚐 American Limo, WLL Limo downtown, $6-6.50; North Milwaukee & suburbs, $9-13.50; West Milwaukee & suburbs, $9-12.50.

🚌 No. 80 bus every 15-50 min M-F 5:50 am-9:58 pm. Sat every 30 min from 7:09 am to 6:13 pm. Sun-Hol 11:50 am, 12:41 pm and approx every 30 min to 5:45 pm. $1 fare—bills OK. 35-min ride to 6th & Wisconsin downtown. Picks up at shelter at far right (north) end of ramp outside terminal.

**To O'Hare & Midway airports, Chicago** United Limo every 2 hrs 4:15 am-8:15 pm. 1 hr 45 min, $10 OW, $15 RT to O'Hare; 2 hr 35 min, $10 addl OW to Midway. Info: 414-747-1666. Greyhound to O'Hare, $9 OW, $15 RT. Info:414-272-2954. **To Madison** Madison Express: noon, 6:30 pm. $19.95. Info: 800-236-4655.

🚗 Alamo, Avis, Budget, Dollar, Hertz, National, Thrifty.

**P** ST $7, LT $2.

# MINNEAPOLIS/ST. PAUL, Minnesota
Minneapolis-St. Paul Intl Airport, 13 mi SE of Minneapolis, 8 mi SW of St. Paul

🚕 **To Mpls** $18, 20-30 min. **To St. Paul** $14, 20-25 min. Others: Wayzata $30; Bloomington $14; 3M, $19; General Mills $26; Control Data $8.

🚐 **To Mpls** Minneapolis Airport Limousine every 15-20 min from lower level 5:30 am-midnight. $6.50 OW, $9.50 RT. 30-min ride to downtown hotels. **To St. Paul** St. Paul & Suburban Limousine Service every 20 min. $6.50 OW, $9.50 RT. To Ramada, Howard Johnson, Sheraton, Radisson St. Paul, Radisson Plaza, Travel Lodge, Holiday, others by reservation: 612-726-5479. **To Eau Claire, Menomonie, Hudson** Eau Claire Passenger Service: 715-835-0399. **To Rochester** Jefferson Lines: 612-371-3311. Rochester Express: 507-288-4490. **To Marshall, Watertown, Glenwood, Morris, Rice Lake, Hayward, Ashland, Ironwood** Four Star Lines: 612-537-0604.

🚌 **To Mpls** No. 7 bus from heated shelter at right end of lower level. 5:09 am-12:10 am M-F every 20-40 min, every 60-min Sat-Sun-Hol. 90¢ peak times, 75¢ otherwise. 42 min to Hennepin & Washington downtown. No. 35P Express M-F to city at 6:38, 7:12, 7:26, 7:52 am; from city at 3:31, 4:35, 5:15, 5:32 pm. $1. To 2nd Ave. & 2nd St. **To St. Paul** Take No. 7 (above), transfer at Ft. Snelling to No. 9 for downtown. 30 min. No. 62 Express inbound at 3:43, 3:53, 4:03, 4:23, 4:33 pm. Outbound from 6th & Wabash at 7:36, 7:52, 8:04, 8:19, 8:34 am. 22-min run. $1.

🚗 Avis, Budget, Dollar, Hertz, National. To cut traffic circling in front of terminal, a common "Rental Auto Shuttle Bus" has replaced individual company buses, adding a few minutes to pick-up and drop-off process.

**P** ST $24.25, LT $10. Remote $6, free shuttle. Off-airport parking may be more convenient during construction. Choices include EZ Air Park, 2804 Lexington, Eagan; MSP Park Place, 2545 Stewart St., St. Paul. Free shuttles.

**Note** Construction of new roads and parking lots may add 20 min travel time to the airport. Work is scheduled to be completed in late 1989. Revised roadway system will both speed access to the terminals and cut carbon monoxide levels outside baggage claim: drivers will have to either park or exit the airport—circling will not be possible.

## MOBILE, Alabama
Mobile Municipal Airport, 15 mi W

🚕 $15 for up to two people, 20¢ each addl. 20-30 min.

🚐 Mobile Bay Limousine 5 am-last flight. $10 to down-town hotels. AMEX.

🚗 Avis, Budget, Dollar, Hertz, National.

## MOLOKAI, Hawaii
Molokai Airport, 8 mi NW of Kaunakakai

🚐 Gray Line: call 567-6177. To Ke Nani Kai, Paniolo Hale, Sheraton Molokai on west end, $6 per person. To Hotel Molokai, Pau Hana Inn on east end, $6 per person, minimum two.

🚗 Avis, Budget, Dollar, Tropical.

## MOMBASA, Kenya
Moi Intl Airport, 8 mi (13 km) W

🚕 KS100 ($6), 15 min; to hotels, KS165 ($10), 20 min. Tip not necessary but KS20 ($1) OK for good service.

🚌 Kenya Bus Service departs terminal every 30 min 5 am-10 pm. Fare to driver KS3 (20¢). Baggage OK. 20 min to central city.

🚗 Avis, Dian, Glory, Kenatco, Ocean, Taxis Coop.

**P** KS1 (6¢)/hour.

## MONTEGO BAY, Jamaica
Sangster Intl Airport, 3 mi (5 km) N

🚕 To city center J$35 ($6.50), 10 min. To resort hotels J$67 ($12.50).

🚗 American Intl, Avis, Budget, Dollar, Greenlight, Hertz,

Island, Jamaica, Liberty, National, Pleasure Tours, Thrifty, United. J$1 (20¢)

## MONTEREY, California
Monterey Peninsula Airport, 3 mi E

🚗 $5-6, 7-10 min.

🚌 No. 21 Salinas bus hourly M-Sat 7:28 am-6:48 pm. 13 min downtown. 75¢.

🚗 Avis, Dollar, Hertz.

## MONTERREY, Mexico
Mariano Escobedo Intl Airport, 12 mi NE

🚗 $7 flat rate, 30 min. Tipping not customary.

🚗 Avis, Budget, Dollar, Hertz, National, Thrifty.

## MONTREAL, Quebec
Dorval Intl Airport, 12 mi (20 km) NW

🚗 C$19 ($15.60), 20-30 min.

🚐 Aerocar bus every 20-30 min 7 am-11:59 pm. C$7 ($5.75), 25 min to downtown hotels: Bonaventure, Le Chateau Champlain, Queen Elizabeth, Centre Sheraton.

🚊 Bus connection via No. 204 Cardinal Est (East), C$1 (80¢). Get a transfer. Change at Dorval Shopping Centre (a 5-min ride) to No. 211. 15-min express ride to Lionel Groulx station. Transfer to Metro for downtown. 45 min total.

**To Mirabel Airport** Aerocar hourly 10:20 am-10:20 pm. C$9 ($7.40), 50 min.

🚗 Avis, Budget, Hertz, Lovec, Thrifty, Tilden.

**P** ST C$8 ($6.55), LT C$6 ($4.90).

**Ski season special** From early December to late March, AEROSKI coach connects Dorval & Mirabel with the ski country: Ste. Adele, Val David, Mt. Blanc, St-Jovite, Gray Rocks, Villa Bellevue, Auberge Cuttles, Manoir Pinoteau, Mont Tremblant. Info: 514-397-9999.

# MOSCOW, USSR
Sheremetyevo Airport, 16 mi (26 km) NW

🚗 Rb5-10 ($1.40-2.75), 40 min to the Kremlin—but only after waiting in cab line for up to 30 min. Tip 10%.

🚌 Hourly shuttle bus to Aeroport station on Metro Line 2. 5-kopeck coin (1¢) through turnstile. Metro runs 6 am-12:30 am. Five stops to Sverdlova Ploshchad—Red Square. Moscow Metro is fast, comfortable, frequent, cheap, and a celebration of Soviet architecture in marble and mosaic. No fun if you are laden with luggage, however.

🚙 Intourist makes arrangements.

# MT. HAGEN, Papua New Guinea
Kagamuga Airport, 7 mi (11 km) NE

🚗 No taxis.

🚐 PMV—public motor vehicle—is a cross between minibus and truck. Not elegant but practical and cheap. 15-20 min, 30toea (35¢) to city center.

🚙 Avis, Budget.

# MUNICH, West Germany
Munich-Riem Airport, 6 mi (10 km) SE

🚗 DM22 ($11.70), 30 min to city center. Tip unnecessary, but for good service a few marks.

🚌 Munich Airport City Service bus every 15-20 min 6 am-9:30 pm but meets flights outside these hours. DM5 ($2.70) to Hauptbahnhof (main station), where cabs are available. 20-25 min.

🚌 No. 91 from stop between terminals to Riem Station of U-Bahn (metro). Transfer to train S-1. DM3.60 ($1.90) bus fare includes transfer to U-Bahn.

🚗 Autohansa, Avis, Bach-Taxi, Europcar, Eurorent, Hertz, InterRent, Mages-Autovermietung, Schuldt, Sixt.

**P** ST DM25 ($13.50), LT DM11 ($5.85).

## NADI, Fiji
Nadi Intl Airport, 5 mi (8 km) NE of Nadi, 90 mi (146 km) NW of Suva

🚗 F$4 ($3.20), 12 min. To Sigatoka, F$35 ($28), 2 hrs.

🚗 Avis, A-Team, Budget, Hertz, Khans, National, Roxy, Thrifty.

## NAIROBI, Kenya
Jomo Kenyatta Airport, 10 mi (16 km) SE

🚗 Ksh180 ($11), 15 min. Tip optional.

🚌 Kenya Bus Service No. 34 hourly 6:30 am-8 pm. Ksh6 (40¢). Baggage OK. 30 min to city center.

🚗 Ark Travel, Avis, Europcar (Airporter), Hertz/UTC, Kenatco, Jambo Taxis.

## NANTUCKET, Massachusetts
Nantucket Airport, 3 mi SE

🚗 $6, 7 min. To beach, $5, 5 min. Extra passengers, $1 each.

🚗 Avis, Budget, Hertz, National, Thrifty.

**P** ST $7.50, LT $4.50.

## NAPLES, Florida
Naples Municipal Airport, 3 mi NE

🚕 $6, 5 min. To Beach Club Hotel, $8.50, 10 min; Ritz-Carlton, $15.50, 20 min; Registry, $12, 15 min. Addl passengers $1 each. Baggage 50¢ each.

🚗 Avis, Hertz, National.

**P** Free.

## NAPLES, Italy
Capodichino Airport, 4 mi (7 km) N

🚕 Lit15,000-20,000 ($11.25-15) includes empty return, 30 min. Tip 10%.

🚗 Autotravel, Avis, Budget, Europcar, Euro-Rent, Eurotrans, Hertz, InterRent, Italy by Car, Maggiore.

**P** Lit10,000 ($7)/day.

## NASHVILLE, Tennessee
Nashville Metropolitan Airport, 10 mi SE

🚕 $12-14, addl riders 50¢ each. 15-45 min depending on traffic.

🚗 Alamo, American Intl, Avis, Budget, Dollar, Hertz, National, Payless, Snappy, Thrifty.

## NASSAU, Bahamas
Nassau Intl Airport, 12 mi (19 km) SW

🚕 $10, 25-30 min to Nassau.

🚗 Avis, Budget, National.

# NEW ORLEANS, Louisiana
New Orleans Intl Airport, 14 mi W

🚕 $18 flat rate downtown for up to 3 people, $6 addl for 4. 30-40 min.

🚐 Orleans Transportation, $7 to downtown, French Quarter hotels. **To Slidell, Biloxi** Coastliner van at 8:30, 10:30 am; noon, 1:30, 3:30, 5:30, 7:30, 9:30, 11:30 pm. Slidell, $18 OW, $30 RT, 60 min; Biloxi, $29 OW, $50 RT, 2-1/2 hr. Reservations required: (US) 800-647-3957, (Miss) 800-622-3022.

🚌 Airport-Downtown Express 5:30 am-5:40 pm M-F at 10-20 min intervals, 30-60 min until 11:30 pm. Sat-Sun-Hol on a 20-40 min schedule. $1.10 exact coins. 50-min ride to Elk Pl. downtown. **To Gulfport Municipal Airport** See Coastliner listing at limos, above.

🚗 Alamo, American Intl, Avis, Budget, Dollar, Enterprise, Hertz, National, Payless, Snappy, Thrifty.

**P** ST $12, LT $4.

# NEW YORK, New York
Kennedy Intl Airport, 15 mi SE

**Toll Free U.S. Number** for Kennedy, LaGuardia, Newark ground transportation information: 800-AIR-RIDE.

🚕 $24-30 plus tolls, 35-60 min to Manhattan. To LaGuardia $18.

🚐 Carey Coach every 30 min 6 am-midnight. $8 fare to driver, 45 min to 42nd St. opposite Grand Central Terminal, Grand Hyatt Hotel. 60 min to Port Authority Bus Terminal. Connection at 42nd St. for New York Hilton, Sheraton City Squire, Marriott Marquis. Comfortable. **To major Manhattan hotels** Abbeys Transportation,

Giraldo Limousine. $11 per person, 60 min. Reserve at Ground Transportation Center.

🚁 New York Helicopter 10:05 am, then every 30 min 1:45-7:15 pm. 10 min to E 34 St heliport. $58—some airlines offer free connection. Boards at TWA gate 37. Info: 800-645-3494.

🚆 JFK Express every 20 min 6:03 am-12:52 am. Take free shuttle bus from each terminal to Howard Beach Station. Train fare $6.50. Eight stops in Brooklyn, Manhattan. Scheduled 48-min ride to terminus, 57th St. & Avenue of the Americas, midtown. To return to JFK, pay $1 to enter subway, addl $5.50 aboard JFK Express. This is a clean, safe, swift way to get into town. A/C coaches, transit police aboard, plenty of baggage space. Commuter booklets of 20 tickets sold at Howard Beach for $50.

🚌 Q10 bus with transfer to A, E, or F subway. Bus every 15-30 min, $1 exact fare or token. Transfer at Lefferts Blvd for A train to lower Manhattan/financial district during daytime. Evening hours, ride to end of line at Kew Gardens-Union Turnpike, transfer to E or F train for midtown. Subway addl $1 or token. (Cheapest way to Manhattan but not recommended if you're laden with luggage.)

**To LIRR Jamaica Station** Carey Coach every 30 min 5:30 am-11 pm. $4. 30-min trip. Bus continues to LaGuardia. **To Jamaica** Q3 bus every 15-30 min 5:10 am-1:40 am. $1 exact fare or token. 35 min to 165 St bus terminal. **To LaGuardia** Carey Coach every 30 min 5:30 am-11 pm. $7. See Jamaica LIRR, above. **To Newark Intl** Salem Trans. Several morning runs, hourly 1:30-7:30 pm. 75-min trip, $18. Info: NJ 800-624-4274, NY 718-656-4511.

🚗 Avis, Budget, Dollar, Hertz, National.

**P** ST $24, LT $5. Free, 24-hour shuttle every 10 min peak hours, every 30 min late night to remote lot.

**See New York-LaGuardia listing for services to Long Island, Connecticut, New Jersey**

# NEW YORK, New York
LaGuardia Airport, 8 mi NE

**Toll Free U.S. Number** for Kennedy, LaGuardia, Newark airport ground transportation information: 800-AIR-RIDE.

🚗 $15-17 to midtown Manhattan plus tolls. 20-40 min. Two or more people can split cost on Share-a-Ride (except Sat, Hol). Groups form at dispatch area just outside baggage claim. To JFK, $18, 20-30 min. **Questions?** Ask at Ground Transportation Center at each baggage claim area.

🚌 Carey Coach every 20-30 min 6:45 am-midnight. $6 fare to driver, 30-45 min ride. Stops on 42nd St. opposite Grand Central Terminal, Grand Hyatt Hotel; New York Hilton at Rockefeller Center; Sheraton City Squire; Marriott Marquis. Transfer at 42nd St. to Port Authority Bus Terminal. Comfortable. **To Major Manhattan hotels** Abbeys Transportation, Giraldo Limousine. $8 per person, 45 min. Reserve at Ground Transportation Center.

🚌 Q-33 to end of line, Roosevelt Ave-Jackson Hts, $1 exact or token. Clean coaches, baggage space. Service all times, 15-60 min frequency from bus stop all terminals. 20-min ride through tidy Queens neighborhoods. Transfer to E subway for Port Authority Bus Terminal, Penn Station, World Trade Ctr; or F subway for Rockefeller Center, Washington Sq, Lower East Side.

Or take No. 7 Flushing elevated to Grand Central. Transfer costs $1 or token. 10-20 min to Manhattan.

**To Wall St.** Pan Am Water Shuttle, M-F only. Take free Pan Am shuttle bus every 15 min to boat dock at Marine Air Terminal. Inbound boats at 7:45, 8:45, 9:45 am; 4:45, 5:45, 6:45 pm. 35 min by water to Pier 11, corner Wall St. & South St. Outbound at 8:45 am; 3:45, 4:45, 5:45 pm. Intermediate stop at 35th St. & East River. $20 OW, $38 RT.

**To Jamaica Station LIRR** Carey Coach every 30 min 6:30 am-11 pm. $4. 30-min run. Bus continues to JFK, arriving 15-20 min later. Fare LaGuardia-JFK, $7.

**To Kennedy Intl Airport** See Carey Coach listing to Jamaica Station LIRR, above. **To Newark Intl Airport** Salem Transportation Sun-Fri service every 2 hrs on the half hour 7:30 am-7:30 pm. $17.

🚗 Avis, Budget, Dollar, Hertz, National.

**P** $15/day. **To Nassau, Suffolk counties** Airlimo Long Island operates 5 am-2 am. Fares $7-21. Request service at Ground Transportation Center. Shared door-to-door service available. Res: 516-872-4754. Also Transport Limousine of Long Island. Res: 800-832-5466 (NY); 800-645-1164 (US). **To Connecticut** Connecticut Limousine to Danbury, New Haven, Bridgeport, Norwalk, Hartford, Stamford and surrounding towns. Frequent scheduled service 8 am-midnight. Fares $20-25. Info: 718-656-5262, 800-2436152 (NY) or inquire at Ground Transportation Center. **To Westchester and Upstate New York** Connecticut Limousine, 800-243-6152, 914-699-1000; Flightcatches-Shortline, 800-631-8405, 201-529-3666; Leprechaun Skylink, 800-321-5465; 914-896-4600. **Shared door-to-door service available:** Westchester Express, 212-431-4400, 914-667-2400.

# NEWARK, New Jersey

Newark Intl Airport, 16 mi SW of midtown New York City

**Toll Free US Number** for Newark, LaGuardia, Kennedy ground transportation information: 800-AIR-RIDE.

🚗 $28-30 plus tolls ($3-4), 30-45 min to midtown Manhattan. Flat rates: to Newark Hilton, Penn Station (downtown) $12, 15 min; to LaGuardia $38.50; JFK $47.50; Atlantic City $119. Group rates to Manhattan 8 am to midnight, split cost, four passengers maximum.

🚌 Olympia Trails Express Bus to World Trade Center, Grand Central Stn every 20 min 5 am-1 am. Pay driver $7. From North Terminal (last airport stop) to World Trade, 20 min; Grand Central, 35 min.

🚌 NJ Transit No. 300 Express to Port Authority Bus Terminal, 8th Ave. & 42nd St. Every 15-30 min 24 hrs a day. 30-45 min travel time. Pay driver $7. Both buses pick up at arrivals levels all terminals. Driver stows baggage below. Comfortable ride.

🚌 Giraldo Minibus to any Manhattan address between 14th & 90th St. Schedules vary with demand. Fare $12-18. Travel time about 55 min. Buy ticket at Ground Transportation Center.

🚋 Airlink No. 302 bus connects airport with PATH and Amtrak trains in Newark Penn Station. Every 20-30 min 6 am-2 am. $4. Baggage racks, comfortable. 15-min ride. Cheaper: No. 62 NJ Transit bus from terminals A,B,C (but not North Terminal) every 30 min peak times, 60 min otherwise. 85¢. Baggage room, comfortable. 15 min from Terminal C to Newark station.

🚋 PATH trains from Track 1 Newark Penn Station to **World Trade Center**, lower Manhattan. $1 fare, coins or bill, in turnstile. Very frequent service rush hours M-F, 6-10 min frequencies midday, 20-30 min late night. Trains extremely crowded rush hours. Info: 201-963-2558. NJ Transit or Amtrak trains to **Penn Station, Manhattan** every 5-25 min 6:15 am-11:55 pm, also 12:55, 2:38 am. Buy ticket in advance, $1.75. About a 15-min ride.

**To JFK airport:** Salem Transportation, Sun-Fri service every hour on the half hour 7:30 am-5:30 pm. $18. Info: NJ 800-624-4274; NY 718-656-4511.

🚗 Airways, Avis, Budget, Dollar, Hertz, National.

**P** ST $24 first day, $48 second and succeeding days. LT $12, $5. Parking for up to 24 hrs can be prepaid in baggage claim of terminals A, B. Saves time on way out. **To Connecticut, Westchester County, NY** Connecticut Limousine hourly service 7:45 am-11:45 pm, 1 am, to New Haven, Bridgeport, Norwalk, Stamford, Greenwich, New Rochelle. Reserve at Ground Transportation Counter. Fares $19-26. **To Atlantic City** Greyhound at 8, 10:20 am; 12:01, 1, 2, 4, 7, 9 pm. 2 hr 20 min run. $12. Purchase ticket at booth in Terminal B or from driver. Info: 201-642-8205. **To other points in NJ** Airport Limousine Express, 201-621-7300; Airport Jet Express, 201-961-2501; Princeton Airporter, 800-451-0246; Salem Transportation, 201-961-4250. :bTo Upstate NY Leprechaun Skylink, 800-321-5465.

**Ridgewood Satellite Parking Lot** To relieve traffic at airport and save travellers' nerves and money, the airport is promoting a new satellite terminal in Ridgewood, NJ, on Rte. 17 South just north of the Garden State Parkway. Parking $2/day in fenced, guarded lot. Shuttle to airport aboard Air Brook Express, $12, departs every 30 min 5:30 am-11 pm. 45-min ride. Return from airport same fare and frequency, 6 am-1 am.

# NICE, France
Nice/Cote d'Azur Airport, 4 mi (7 km) W

🚕 F80-100 ($13-16) to centre ville for 3 passengers, 4 only if driver agrees. Extra for luggage F5 apiece. Tip 10-15% for special service. 10-30 min depending on traffic. Surcharges Sun, Hol.

🚌 Special Aeroport express runs along Promenade des Anglais coast road. Look for BUS signs on wall at west Terminal 1 exit. Pay fare F15 ($2.50) aboard. Service from 6:10 am (7:10 Sun) to 11:10 pm, at 20-25 min intervals peak hours, 30-60 min other times. Small bus, little room for luggage. Some services call at SNCF railway station in Nice by request. Gare Routiere Departmentale (Central Coach Station) is end of the line. 15-35 min.

Frequent minibus service to **Cannes, Monaco,** and other nearby coastal points. Inquire at Airport Information office.

🚌 No. 9 bus stops across road and to left of express coach described above. Pay F5.80 ($1) aboard. No baggage space and may be quite crowded during peak hour commutes. Follows inland route, numerous stops. 45-50 min to Place Massena & Ave. Jean Medecin. Inbound, bus is marked PORT; outbound, AEROPORT.

🚗 Airport Autos, Avis, Budget/Milleville, Citer, Europcar, Hertz, InterRent, Mattei, Sporting Intl.

**P** F49 ($8).

# NORFOLK, Virginia
Norfolk Intl Airport, 6 mi NE

🚕 $15, 15-25 min to Norfolk; $28, 20 min to Virginia Beach. To Williamsburg, $70 flat for up to 5 people, 45 min.

🚐 Airport Limousine Service, $5.25 to Norfolk; $8.75 to Virginia Beach; $18.50 to Williamsburg. Hourly service every day to last flight.

🚌 Avis, Budget, Dollar, Hertz, National.

# OAKLAND, California
Oakland Intl Airport, 11 mi SE of Oakland, 19 mi SE of San Francisco

🚗 Oakland, $16-17, 10-15 min. San Francisco, $30-35, 25-60 min plus $1 bridge toll Sun-Th, $2 F-Sat.

🚆 Take Air-BART shuttle from shelter on center island to left outside entrance. Every 5 min, 6 am-midnight M-Sat (from 9 am Sun). Baggage rack inside. $1, 10-min ride to Coliseum station of BART. To Oakland City Center-12th St. take Richmond train. 80¢, 11 min. To downtown San Francisco, take Daly City train, $1.90, 21-27 min to Embarcadero, Montgomery, Powell, Civic Center stations. BART is clean, quiet, fast. Plenty of information, easy to use.

🚌 AC Transit No. 61 to downtown Oakland M-F every 30-60 min 5:51 am-7:42 pm. 75¢, 30 min to 12th & Franklin.

**To San Francisco Intl Airport (SFO)** Bay Area Bus Service Airporter departs hourly on the hour 6 am-midnignt. $7, 60 min to SFO. Each run begins at Hyatt Regency, Oakland, 15 min before Oakland departure.

🚌 Alamo, Avis, Budget, Dollar, Hertz, National, Snappy, Thrifty, Ugly Duckling.

**P** ST $10, LT $5. Free shuttle every 5 min.

**To Travis AFB, Fairfield** Travis Express. Info: 707-437-3386. **To Pleasanton, Dublin, San Ramon, Castro Valley**

San Ramon Valley Airporter Express. Res: 415-484-4044.
**To Napa, Vallejo** Grapevine Airport Service. Res: 707-253-9093.

## OKLAHOMA CITY, Oklahoma
Will Rogers World Airport, 11 mi SW

🚗 $12, $1 each addl rider. 20 min.

🚐 Airport Express shared-ride vans. $6 first person, $3 each addl to downtown hotels. Leaves from lower level adjacent to baggage claim. AMEX, MC, VISA.

🚙 Alamo, Avis, Budget, Dollar, Enterprise, Hertz, National, Snappy, Thrifty.

**P** ST $8, LT $4-5.

## OMAHA, Nebraska
Eppley Airport, 5 mi NE

🚗 $5-6, 5-10 min.

🚐 $5-6. Call 342-1131 if station wagon is not at airport.

🚙 American Intl, Avis, Budget, Dollar, Enterprise, Hertz, National, Snappy, Thrifty.

**P** ST $12, LT $3.

## ONTARIO, California
Ontario Intl Airport, 22 mi SW of San Bernardino; 17 mi NW of Riverside; 11 mi E of Pomona; 41 mi E of downtown Los Angeles

🚗 Pomona $16, 25 min; Riverside $32-35, 40 min; San Bernardino/ Loma Linda $40, 45 min; Los Angeles (LAX) $85-90, 75-90 min. **To downtown LA** SuperShuttle $50 first passenger, $60 for group up to 7.

🚐 **To Palm Desert, Palm Springs, Riverside, San Bernardino** Airportcoach 800-772-5299, 714-527-1992. Boards along sidewalk to right outside terminal past Avis car return.

🚌 No. 496 RTD bus loads to right along sidewalk past car return. Eastbound service to San Bernardino/ Riverside. Westbound to LA. M-F at 5:58, 7:03, 8:22 am, then hourly at :36 to 3:36 pm; then 4:38, 5:38, 6:38, 7:33 pm. 75-min run to 7th & Maple, downtown LA. $2.75. Slower service to LA on RTD No. 484. To Disneyland, Knotts Berry Farm, RTD No. 149.

**To LAX** Airportcoach at 6:30, 10:15 am; 3:00, 8:00 pm. $12, 75-90 min. Return from LAX at 9:00 am; 1:15, 7:00, 9:45 pm. Also SuperShuttle $38 first passenger, $6 each addl.

🚗 Avis, Budget, Dollar, Hertz, National.

**P** ST $5.25, LT $2.75.

## ORANGE COUNTY, California
John Wayne Airport, 5 mi S of Santa Ana; 5 mi NE of Newport Beach; 10 mi SE of Disneyland/Anaheim Convention Center

🚗 Newport Beach, $13-16; Anaheim/Disneyland, $23-24; U.C. Irvine, $7; Santa Ana, $14; Costa Mesa, $8; Los Angeles Intl (LAX), $61 flat rate.

🚐 **To Disneyland/Anaheim** SuperShuttle, $10 to hotels. **Orange County door-to-door** SuperShuttle, $33 first person, $6 each addl. Res: 714-973-1100. **To Anaheim** Airport Coach, approx hourly 8:20 am-10 pm. 25 min to Anaheim terminal, free transfer to hotels. $4 adults, $2 kids.

🚌 OCTD Bus No. 61 to Santa Ana, Newport Beach, approx hourly service 5:55 am-6:03 pm M-F. 80. Surfboards 6 ft or under OK. **To Los Angeles Intl, Long Beach airports** SuperShuttle to LAX $15; to LGB $32. Prepayment required when reservation is made; AMEX, MC, VISA accepted. Res & info: 714-973-1100.

🚗 Avis, Hertz, Budget.

**P** ST $15, LT (Main Street), $5. Free shuttle every 15 min.

## ORANJESTAD, Aruba
Queen Beatrix Intl Airport, 2 mi (1.25 km) E

🚕 $6 flat rate, 7-10 min. To hotels on W coast, $8, 15-20 min. Baggage $1. Tip $1-2. (US currency is as readily accepted as the Aruban florin.)

🚌 ARUBUS picks up 5-min walk from airport, hourly 7 am-7 pm. 85¢ 10-15 min to Oranjestad. Small baggage OK.

🚗 Avis, Budget, Dollar, Hertz, InterRent, J/M, Marco's, National.

**P** $4.60/day.

## ORLANDO, Florida
Orlando Intl Airport, 12 mi SE of Orlando, 23 mi NE of Disneyworld

🚕 $15-20, 20 min to Orlando; $30-32, 35 min to Disneyworld.

🚐 Airport Limousine $9 OW, $16 RT to Orlando; $11 OW, $20 RT to Disneyworld. AMEX, MC, VISA at airport only.

🚌 No. 11 bus hourly 5:45 am-9:20 pm. 75¢. 40 min to Pine St. terminal, downtown.

🚗 Alamo, American Intl, Avis, Budget, Dollar, Hertz, National, Payless, Snappy, USA.

**P** ST $24, LT $3.

## OSAKA, Japan
Osaka Intl Airport, 10 mi (17 km) NE

🚕 Y4500 ($33.30), 30-45 min downtown. To Kyoto, Y13,700 ($101), 50 min; to Kobe, Y8250 ($61).

🚌 Osaka Airport Transport Co. every 15 min 8 am-8 pm. Y380 ($2.80). 35-45 min downtown Osaka. To Kyoto, Y800 ($6); to Kobe, Y620 ($4.60).

🚗 Avis, Hertz.

## OSLO, Norway
Fornebu Airport, 6.25 mi (10 km) W

🚕 NKr80 ($12), 20-25 min. Tip 10%.

🚌 SAS bus from outside arrivals hall to Central Railway Station (harbor side), Hotel Scandinavia, Braathen SAFE Terminal at Haakon VII St. Departures every 15 min 7:30 am (8 Sun) to 11:30 pm. Pay driver NKr20 ($3). 20-25 min ride. On Sat evening, Sun, bus runs every 30 min. Info phone: 42 49 41.

🚌 Bus No. 31 outside arrival hall. NKr10 ($1.50) to driver. Departures every 15-30 min 6:08 am-12:08 am. No special baggage space. Many stops into town: 30-35 min ride.

Note: Although Fornebu Airport receives most international and all domestic traffic, increasing numbers of flights will be shifted to the new international airport, **Gardermoen, 33 mi (53 km) NE**.

🚗 NKr450 ($67), 50 min.

🚌 New York Expressen bus meets flights, NKr50 ($7.50).

🚘 Avis, Budget/Hasco, Europcar, Hertz/Kjoles, InterRent.

P ST: NKr40 ($6), LT: NKr30 ($4.50).

## OTTAWA, Ontario
Ottawa Intl Airport, 5 mi S

🚗 C$14-15 ($11.50-12.30), 20-30 min.

🚌 Carleton Bus Lines, C$5.50 ($4.50) every 30 min 7 am-11 pm M-F, every 30 min Sat-Sun. 30 min to downtown hotels.

🚘 Avis, Budget, Hertz, Tilden.

## PALERMO, Sicily
Punta Raisi Airport, 18 mi (30 km) NW

🚗 Lit40,000 ($28.65), 40-50 min.

🚌 Hotels Porto Rais, Azzolini Residence, Palm Beach provide free transport.

🚌 Prestia e Comande bus every 60-90 min 5:45 am-last flight. 50 min to Politeama Square. A/C. Baggage OK. Fare to driver Lit3300 ($2.35).

🚘 Avis, Europcar, Hertz, Holiday, InterRent, Italy by Car, Maggiore.

P Lit10,000 ($7.15) first day, Lit6,000 ($4.30) succeeding days.

## PALM SPRINGS, California
Palm Springs Regional Airport, 2 mi E

🚗 $5, 5 min.

🚐 Sunbus, from road in front of terminal. Continuous service 7 am-6:27 pm. Pay driver 50¢. 5 min into city. "Courtesy stops anywhere upon request."

🚗 Alamo, Avis, Budget, Dollar, Hertz, National, Thrifty.

P ST $8/day during peak season Feb-Apr, otherwise $5. LT Open peak season only, $5.


## PALMA, Mallorca
Palma de Mallorca Airport, 7 mi (11.3 km) SE

🚕 Pta1000 ($7.85), 20 min.

🚌 No. 17 every 30-60 min 7:05 am-12:05 am. 30 min to Plaza de Espana, city center.

🚗 Europcar, Hertz, InterRent/Atesa, Regent.


## PANAMA CITY, Florida
Bay County Airport, 5 mi NW

🚕 $7, 15 min. To Panama City Beach, $17.

🚗 Avis, Budget, Dollar, Hertz, National, Snappy, Thrifty.


## PAPEETE, Tahiti
Faaa Airport, 2.5 mi (4 km) W

🚕 F800 ($8), 7 min. Beachcomber Hotel, F500 ($5), 3 min; Maeva Beach Hotel, F500 ($5), 4 min; Tahara'a Hotel, F1400 ($14), 25 min. Baggage F50 (50¢). No tip.

🚐 Le Truck—a jitney with wooden benches—provides colorful, cheap ride into Papeete or anywhere else on the island. To town, about 100 francs (90¢).

🚗 Avis, Europcar, Sotavi-Hertz, Pacificar

# PARIS, France

Charles de Gaulle Airport, 15 mi (25 km) NE

🚕 F140 ($22). After 8 pm, F160 ($25). F3 (45¢) each bag. 45-60 min ride. Tip 10%. Note that some cabs have limit of 3 passengers— could be awkward with party of 4+.

🚌 Air France bus from Aerogare 1 gates 34 & 36, Aerogare 2 gates A5 & B6. Every 12 min 6 am-11 pm. F36 ($5.65), 30-45 min to Porte Maillot (Palais des Congres). Comfortable, ample baggage room, available to passengers on all airlines.

🚌 No. 350 to Gare du Nord, Gare de l'Est, No. 351 to Place de la Nation. Stops Aerogare 1 at RATP sign on Boutiquaire level; Aerogare 2A Gate A5; 2B Gate B6. Fare 6 Metro tickets, F30 ($4.70), if purchased aboard. Packets of 10 Metro tickets purchased in advance also F30 ($4.70). No. 350 every 15 min, No.351 every 30 min, 5:30 am-11 pm. 50-min ride. Many stops, poor baggage space.

🚆 Shuttle bus every 5 min to Roissy Rail from Gate 28 Aerogare 1; gates A5, B6 Aerogare 2. Buy rail ticket at airport before boarding shuttle. To Gare du Nord, 2nd Class F23 ($3.75); 1st Class F35 ($5.70). 35-min ride. Comfortable, plenty of baggage space.

**To Orly** Air France bus from Gate 36, Aerogare 1; Gate A3, B10, Aerogare 2. Every 20 min, F62 ($9.70). 75-min ride.

🚗 Avis, Budget, Cartransit, Citer, Europcar, Hertz, InterRent, Sodexa.

**P** ST F60 ($9.80), LT F35 ($5.70). Weekend rate from 1:30 pm Fri to 1 pm Mon, F120 ($19.60). Free shuttle LT parking from Gate 30 Aerogare 1, gates A5, B6 Aerogare 2.

## PARIS, France
Orly Airport (Sud and Ouest), 8 mi (14 km) S

🚕 F90 ($14) plus F3 (50¢) per bag. 30-45 min to Opera. Fare F110 ($17.25) after 8 pm. Some cabs have a limit of 3 passengers—could be problem with party of 4+.

🚐 Air France coach, F29 ($4.50). Party of 3, F73 ($11.50); party of 4, F89 ($14). Board at Orly Sud Gate J, Orly Ouest Gate E, arrival level. Service every 12 min 5:50 am-11 pm. 30-45 min to Porte d'Orleans, Gare Montparnasse, where there are Metro connections; then Gare des Invalides, connection to RER rail. Comfortable, baggage space, available to passengers on all airlines.

🚌 ORLYBUS to Place Denfert-Rochereau, a Metro connection. Every 15 min 6:30 am-10 pm, then 10:30, 11, 11:30 pm. Fare F18 ($2.80), 40-min run. Travelers with light luggage who know Paris will find this service a way to avoid possible traffic delays on Air France bus to Invalides. Departs Orly from Porte F, Sud Terminal; Porte R, Ouest Terminal.

🚊 Take shuttle to Orly Rail from Sud Gate H, Ouest Gate F, arrivals level. Buy Metro ticket at airport before boarding shuttle: 2nd Class F20 ($3.25); 1st Class F29.20 ($4.75). Shuttles frequent, trains every 15-35 min 5:30 am-11:15 pm to Gare d'Austerlitz with several stops en route. Comfortable, ample baggage space.

**To Charles de Gaulle Airport** Air France bus departs Sud Porte B, Ouest Porte D every 20 min. F62 ($9.70), 75 min.

🚗 Avis, Budget, Citer, Europcar, Hertz, InterRent.

**P** ST F60 ($9.80), LT F35 ($5.70). Free shuttle from Sud Porte H, Ouest Porte F.

# PENANG (GEORGETOWN), Malaysia
Penang Intl Airport, 11 mi (17.6 km) SW

🚕 RGT17 ($6.80), 35 min.

🚗 Avis, Budget, Hertz, National, Sintat.

# PENSACOLA, Florida
Pensacola Regional Airport, 5 mi N

🚕 $7, 50¢ each addl passenger. 15 min.

🚗 Avis, Budget, Dollar, Hertz, National, Snappy, Thrifty.

# PEORIA, Illinois
Peoria Municipal Airport, 5 mi SW

🚕 $9.15, flat rate, addl passengers 20¢ each. 20 min.

🚗 Avis, Budget, Dollar, Hertz, National.

# PERTH, Australia
Perth Airport, 7 mi NE

🚕 A$11.50 ($8) from intl terminal; A$8.50 ($6) from domestic terminal. 15-20 min. To Freemantle, A$20 ($14), 45 min; Scarbrough, A$20 ($14), 45 min; South Perth, A$10 ($7), 20 min. Tip: Passenger discretion.

🚌 Skybus Airport Coach meets flights. A$5 ($3.50) to hotels in city center, 15-20 min.

🚗 Avis, Budget, Hertz, Thrifty.

**P** A$1 (70¢) upon entry covers parking at intl terminal.

# PHILADELPHIA, Pennsylvania
Philadelphia Intl Airport, 8 mi SW

🚕 $18, addl riders 20¢ each. 15-30 min.

🚐 Door-to-door shared ride. Look for "LIMO On Demand Service" to right outside baggage claim. $6 to Center City hotels, $8 to other addresses. 15-30 min.

🚆 AIRPORT rail to Center City. Well marked—follow signs. Every 30 min 6:10 am-12:10 am. $4. Stops at: **30th St. Station:** Amtrak connections to Trenton, New York City, Harrisburg, Pittsburgh, Wilmington, Baltimore, Washington. Station is near U. of Penna., Drexel, Civic Center. **Penn Center:** Business district, hotels, City Hall. **Market East:** Historic district— Independence Hall, Liberty Bell, Betsy Ross House. **Temple U, Broad St. North** Travel time airport-Penn Center, 25 min.

🚗 Avis, Budget, Dollar, Hertz, National.

**P** ST $18, LT $12, Overseas/Remote $6. Shuttle every 5 min.

**To Cherry Hill, Atlantic City** Rapid Rover Airport Shuttle. To Cherry Hill $15.50; Atlantic City $52.50, 3+ passengers $17.50 each. Info: 609-428-1500. **To Wilmington area** Wilmington Shuttle, 302-655-8878.

## PHOENIX, Arizona
Phoenix Sky Harbor Intl Airport, 4 mi SE

🚕 $8-10, 10-15 min to Phoenix; Scottsdale, $8-15. Cabs have various rates; ask driver.

🚐 SuperShuttle (and other) vans provide shared-ride service. Rates vary. Typical: Phoenix $5, Sun City $12, Mesa $12, Scottsdale $10-12, Tempe $5. Confirm with driver. Boarding areas outside baggage claim Terminal 3 and at ground transportation building between Terminal 2 & Intl Terminal. SuperShuttle accepts AMEX, VISA, MC.

🚌 No. 2E bus every 30 min M-F 6 am-6:40 pm from Terminal 3, Executive Terminal. 24 min downtown. 75¢ exact change.

🚗 Ajax, Alamo, American Intl, Avis, Budget, Dollar, General, Hertz, National, Payless, Rent-a-Dent, Value.

**P** ST $10, LT $3. Free shuttle to remote lot every 10-15 min, 30 min late night.

## PITTSBURGH, Pennsylvania
Greater Pittsburgh Intl Airport, 17 mi W

🚗 $27, 25-40 min.

🚍 Airlines Transportation bus from lower level near United baggage claim. Hourly on the hour 9 am-9 pm weekdays. No Sat service. Sun hourly 2 pm-9 pm. $8 to Westin Wm. Penn, Hilton, Sheraton, Hyatt, Vista Intl. Also serves Oakland, Mt. Lebanon, Monroeville. Info: 412-471-2250.

🚗 Avis, Budget, Hertz, National, Payless, Snappy, Thrifty.

**P** ST $15, LT $5.50.

## POINTE-A-PITRE, Guadeloupe
Aeroport Pointe-a-Pitre/Le Raizet, 1.8 mi (3 km) N

🚗 F30 ($5), 10 min; to Gosier, F70 ($11), 20 min; to Sainte-Anne, F100 ($15.70), 35 min; to Bas du Fort, F50 ($7.80), 15 min; to St. Francois, F167 ($26), 45 min. 40% surcharge 8 pm-6 am. Baggage F1.5 (25¢) after first piece; bulky items 3F (50¢) each.

🚌 Co-Transport Society every 20 min 6 am-7 pm. 5F (80¢). 20 min to Pointe-a-Pitre. Baggage OK.

🚗 Avis, Budget, Carpentier, Europcar, Guadeloupe Cars, Hertz, InterRent, Jumbo, Karukera, Soltour.

**P** F6 ($1)/day.

## PORT MORESBY, Papua New Guinea
Jackson Airport, 5 mi (8 km) E

🚕 Metered taxis: K10 ($10), 15-20 min downtown; K5 ($5.50) to Boroko; K7 ($7.70) Waigani. Alternative: PMV—public motor vehicle. Hybrid minibus/truck with wooden benches. They wait on road across parking lot outside terminal. Any trip in Port Moresby costs 30toea (35¢).

🚗 Avis, Budget.

## PORT-AU-PRINCE, Haiti
Mais Gate Airport, 4 mi (6.4 km) NE

🚕 $10, 20 min. To Petion-ville $12, 30 min; Carrefour $14, 45 min. Tip 10%.

🚐 Royal Haitian has a free airport van.

🚗 Avis, Budget, Secom, Toyota.

## PORTLAND, Maine
Portland Intl Jetport, 2 mi SW

🚕 $6, 15 min to intown Portland.

🚌 The Metro every 30 min 7 am-10:20 pm. 75¢ exact change. No Sun service.

🚗 Ajax, Avis, Budget, Hertz, National, Thrifty.

**To Montreal** Greyhound at 2:45, 3:55, 6:15, 8 pm. 2 hr 45 min run. Purchase ticket at Ground Transportation Counter. Info: 802-863-6869.

# PORTLAND, Oregon
Portland Intl Airport, 9 mi NE

🚕 $19-22 downtown, 20 min. Extra passengers, 50¢ each. **Ground transportation info booth** in center of covered waiting area.

🚐 Raztranz (Downtowner) at :15, :35, :55 weekdays, :05, :35 weekends, 5:35-12:05 am. $5 to King's Way, Greyhound, Benson, Hilton, Heathman, Portland, Marriott. 20-40 min. Service to other hotels available subject to space/time. Check with driver. **To hotels/businesses within 4 mi of airport:** Bilix Short Shuttle every 20 min 8 am-12:20 am. $4-7. **To Vancouver:** Vancouver Airporter at :05, 7:05-12:05 am. Downtown, $7.50; Mark 205 Motor Inn, $5; Hazel Bell, $10. 573-9412. **To Gresham, Clackamas, East Multnomah County:** Eastside Airporter at :00, 7 am-12 am. $10. 2-3 passengers to same address, $15. **To Beaverton, Washington Sq, King City, Tigard, Lake Oswego, Tualatin, Wilsonville:** Wilsonville/Tualatin Airporter every 30-60 min 9 am-11:30 pm, $7-15. 692-5222. Beaverton only: Beaverton-Airporter at :15, 7:15-12:15 am. 649-2213. **To Salem** Hut Limo, 363-8059 **To Bend, Redmond** Central Oregon Shuttle. Info:382-9371.

🚌 Tri-Met No. 12 Sandy Blvd. bus every 15-30 min 5:30 am-11:50 pm. First bus Sunday 7:50 am. Pay driver 85¢. Running time to Portland Mall, downtown, 39 min. Bus connects with "Max" trolley downtown & Gresham at Hollywood Transit Center.

🚗 Alamo, American Intl, Avis, Budget, Car Rental 6, Dollar, General, Hertz, National, Payless, Snappy, Thrifty, U-Save.

**P** ST $10, LT $5. Shuttle every 5 min 5:30 am-11 pm, then every 10 min. Remote overflow lot: $3/day. Shuttle every 10 min.

# PRAGUE, Czechoslovakia
Ruzyne Airport, 11 mi (17 km) W

🚕 K480 ($20), 30-60 min depending on traffic. Small surcharge at night. Tip: Round up meter, adding 10%.

🚌 Czechoslovak Airline bus meets flights. Pay K23 (95¢) aboard. Limited baggage space but comfortable 30-40 min ride to Vltava Terminal in Revolucni St. Also CEDOK Shuttle Bus to Parkhotel, Esplanade, Jalta, Ambassador, Panorama, Inter-Continental, Pariz, Alcron, Panorama. Departures at 11 am, 12, 1, 2, 3, 4 pm. K50 ($2). Buy ticket at CEDOK counter No. 29 at airport.

🚌 No. 119 every 10-20 min from outside arrival terminal. Fare K1 (15¢). 35-60 min into town. Stop at Revolucni St. convenient to many hotels. Very limited baggage space. Service 6 am-11 pm. Abbreviated weekend, holiday schedule.

🚗 Pragocar represents Avis, Budget, Denzel, Godfrey Davis/Europcar, Hertz, InterRent.

# PRESTWICK (Glasgow), Scotland
Prestwick Airport, 29 mi (48 km) S of Glasgow

🚕 £21 ($34) into city, no extras. Tip 15%. 45-55 min.

🚌 Scottish Citylink/Dodds Coaches meet intl flights 7:17 am-4:32 pm (Sun 10:12 am and every 2 hrs to 4:12 pm). Pick-up point approx 150 yds from terminal. About 60 min to Glasgow Buchanan Bus Station, connections there to Edinburgh. £2.70 ($4.35).

🚌 No. 04 to Anderson Cross Bus Station every 30 min 5:45 am-10:15 pm. Pay on bus about £2 ($3.20). 90-110 min trip, poor baggage space.

🚇 Railair Link shuttle bus to Prestwick Rail Station operates up to noon or 1 pm most days—to 4:45 pm Th and

2 pm F—and outside these hours by request. 5-min trip. From Prestwick station, trains every 30 min—some pm services hourly—to Glasgow Central Station. First train 7:20 am, last 11:05 pm. 45-min trip. Good baggage space. £2.30 ($3.70).

🚗 Avis, Europcar, Hertz, Swan National/InterRent.

**P** £2.40 ($3.85)/day

# PROVIDENCE, Rhode Island
Theodore Francis Green State Airport, 7 mi S

🚕 $15 flat, 15-20 min.

🚌 Airport Limousine at 60-75 min intervals 5:25 am-12:55 am. $5.75. AMEX, MC, VISA.

🚗 Avis, Budget, Hertz, National, Snappy, Thrifty.

# PUERTO VALLARTA, Mexico
Gustavo Diaz Ordaz Airport, 4 mi (6 km) N

🚕 $3, 10-15 min.

🚌 Colectivos available in front of terminal 8 am-last flight. Drop-off anywhere along route into city. $1.

🚗 Avis, Budget, Dollar, Hertz, National.

# QUEBEC, Quebec
Aeroport de Quebec, 12 mi NW

🚕 C$15-17 ($12-13.60), 25-30 min.

🚌 Old Quebec Tours Inc., C$6.75 ($5.40).

🚗 Avis, Budget, Hertz, Tilden.

# QUEENSTOWN, New Zealand
Frankton Airport, 4.4 mi (7 km) E

🚕 NZ$12 ($7.95), 10 min. Call Southern Taxis 27-888.

🚐 Prestige Airport Shuttle meets flights. NZ$4 ($2.65). 15 min.

🚗 Avis, Budget, Hertz.

## RALEIGH/DURHAM, North Carolina
Raleigh-Durham Airport, 14 mi NW of Raleigh, 6 mi SE of Durham

🚕 To Raleigh $18-20, to Durham $25-27.

🚐 Shannon Transportation, 6:30 am-11:30 pm. $8-12 first person, $4-5 each addl to major hotels, campuses. Res & Info: 919-821-2111. AMEX, MC, VISA.

🚗 Avis, Budget, Dollar, Enterprise, Hertz, National, Snappy, Thrifty.

## REGINA, Saskatchewan
Regina Airport, 5 mi SW

🚕 C$5.50 ($4.50), 10-15 min. Tip 10%. If no cabs at airport, use courtesy phone.

🚗 Avis, Budget, Dollar, Tilden.

**P** C$5 ($4)/day.

## RENO, Nevada
Reno Intl Airport, 3 mi SE

🚕 $7, 7-10 min.

🚐 Airport Limousine, $2.25. 10-15 min to hotels in Reno, Sparks.

🚌 From front of Airport Plaza Hotel. 60¢. 20 min to City Center Transfer.

🚗 Avis, Budget, Dollar, Hertz, National.

## REYKJAVIK, Iceland
Keflavik Airport, 31 mi (50 km) SW

🚌 Bus meets flight. Kr275 ($6), children Kr150 ($3.25). 45 min to hotels Loftleidir, Esja.

🚗 Arnarflug, Avis, Flugleidir

## RICHMOND, Virginia
Richmond Intl Airport, 7 mi SE

🚕 $16-18, addl passengers 30¢ each. 20-30 min.

🚌 Groome Transportation meets flights. Into town: $10.25 one person; $13.75 for two; $16.75 three; $18.50 four; $5.50 each five or more. MC, VISA.

🚗 American Intl, Avis, Budget, Dollar, Hertz, National, Payless, Snappy, Thrifty.

## RIO de JANEIRO, Brazil
Galeao Airport, 12.5 mi (19.3 km) NE

🚕 To city center, CZ3320 ($9.50 — U.S. currency accepted). 25-40 min to Inter-Continental Hotel. Tip 10%. Brazilian officials advise tourists to ignore counter marked "R.D.E." offering assistance with taxis and "passports." Look just beyond for "Rio de Janeiro State Tourism Authority," which sells taxi vouchers at standard rates and offers other legitimate services.

🚌 Airport bus with baggage space, air conditioned (hence called the "Frescao" in Portuguese). Fare to driver CZ600 ($1.70). Departs hourly. Stops at Santos Dumont, the downtown airport, and all beaches and major hotels, terminating at Hotel Nacional in about 1 hr.

🚗 Avis, Budget, Hertz, Localiza, Rentarauto.

P CZ850 ($2.40)/day.

# RIYADH, Saudi Arabia
King Khaled Intl, 17.5 mi (30 km) N

🚗 SR35-75 ($9.30-$20), 35-45 min. Flat rates depend on distance—pay airport cashier in advance. Travelers advised to hire only airport-authorized taxis, identifiable by logo on side of vehicle.

🚌 SAPTCO bus is a luxurious intercity model. Fare SR10 ($2.80). Departures every half hour 6 am-1 am. 50-60 min ride. Stops at Al Batha and some major hotels.

🚗 Avis, Budget, InterRent.

# ROANOKE, Virginia
Roanoke Municipal Airport, 4 mi NW

🚗 $8, addl passengers 20¢ each. 10 min.

🚗 Avis, Budget, Dollar, Hertz, National.

# ROCHESTER, Minnesota
Rochester Municipal Airport, 8 mi S

🚗 $14-15, 15 min.

🚗 Avis, Budget, Hertz, National.

# ROCHESTER, New York
Monroe County Airport, 5 mi SW

🚗 $8-10, addl passengers $2 each. 10-20 min.

🚌 No. 2 Thurston-Parsells bus at 15-30 min intervals 5:50 am-6:33 pm M-F only. 70¢ exact. 28 min to Main & Clinton, downtown.

🚗 Ajax, American Intl, Avis, Budget, Dollar, Hertz, National, Snappy, Thrifty.

# ROME, Italy
Leonardo da Vinci Airport (Fiumicino), 20 mi (32 km) SW

� Lit40,000 ($28.60), 45-60 min to central Rome. Lit500 (40¢) per bag. Fiumicino Guide says, "We strongly advise you to use only licensed taxis with meters and to decline any other offer of transportation." To Rome, fare is meter plus Lit10,000; from Rome, meter plus Lit14,000. Flat fare, no tip.

🚌 Acotral bus: 6:45, 7:15, 7:45 am, then every 15 min to 10:45 pm; 12:15, 12:45 am; hourly 1:15-6:15 am. Buy ticket for Lit5000 ($3.60) at Acotral office outside arrivals area. Plenty of luggage space. Trip to Via Giolitti, at side of Rome RR station, about 55 min. "Easy, quick, great tour of Rome downtown via window of bus," our correspondent writes.

🚗 Avis, Eurodrive, Europcar, Hertz, InterRent/Autotravel, Italy by Car, Maggiore.

**P** ST Lit24,000 ($17.20), LT Lit10,100 ($7.25).

# ROTTERDAM, Netherlands
Zestenhoven Airport, 5 mi N

🚖 Dfl15-20 ($7-9.50), 15 min.

🚌 No. 33 to Central Station about every 30 min. Local service, 25-min ride. Dfl2.50 ($1.20).

🚗 Avis, Budget, Europcar, Hertz.

# SACRAMENTO, California
Metropolitan Airport, 11 mi NW

🚖 $18-19, 15-20 min.

🚐 Skyline Airporter, Downtown Airporter, $5.50 to downtown hotels, 15-20 min. **To Chico, Yuba City, Oroville, Marysville, Paradise** Airport Transportation Service. Res: 916-891-1219. **To Wheatland, Live Oak, Sutter, Beale AFB** Yuba City Airporter Service. Res: 916-671-1199.

🚗 Avis, Budget, Dollar, Hertz, National.

**P** ST $5, LT $3.

## SAGINAW/BAY CITY/MIDLAND, Michigan
Tri City Airport, 10 mi NW of Saginaw, 11 mi SE of Midland, 13 mi SW of Bay City

🚗 $18 flat fare to Saginaw, Bay City, or Midland. 20 min.

🚗 Avis, Budget, Hertz, National, Thrifty.

## SALT LAKE CITY, Utah
Salt Lake City Intl Airport, 6 mi NW

🚗 $9.75, 10-15 min downtown. To Park City $45, Ogden $55, Provo $65, Alta $43.

🚌 **To Park City** Park City Transportation Service, $48 for 1-3 people; 4+, $12 each. **To Ogden, Logan, Hill AFB, Morgan, Roy, Brigham City, Tremonton** Key-North Limousine at 8:30, 11 am; 2, 4, 5:30, 8, 10:30 pm. Sat-Sun-Hol: 8:30, 11 am; 5, 10 pm. $15.75 to Ogden, $41.75 to Logan for one person, $30.75 each two or more.**To Orem, Provo & South** Key Limousine Service. $15.50 to Orem, Provo; $29 to Santaquin. Info: 801-224-4660.

**To ski resorts** Scheduled service available during season. Inquire at ground transportation counter.

🚌 No. 50/150 Airport/Intl Center bus every 30-60 min 6:31 am-11:50 pm M-F. Sat hourly 6:35 am-6:35 pm. Fare 50¢. Limited Sun service, no Hol. Bus stops between terminals 1 & 2. 30-min ride to 355 S. Main St., downtown.

🚙 Ajax, Alamo, American Intl, Auto Express, Avis, Budget, Dollar, Freedom, General, Hertz, Lease-A-Lizzy, National, Payless, Rent-a-Wreck, Snappy.

**P** ST $4.85, LT $2.85. Free shuttle every 5 min.

## SALZBURG, Austria
Salzburg Airport, 4.25 mi (7 km) SW

🚗 S80-90 ($6.20-7) for 3 persons, S5 (40¢) for the fourth. To downtown hotels, 10-15 min. Tip 10%.

🚌 No. 77 every 20 min 5:54 am-11:11 pm to main central station. S12 (95¢), buy ticket on bus. 15 min to Bahnhof. Sunday service less frequent. No room for large baggage.

🚙 Avis, Budget, Denzel, Hertz, InterRent.

**P** S60 ($4.65)/day dropping to S40 ($3.10)/day after 8 days.

## SAN ANTONIO, Texas
San Antonio Intl Airport, 8 mi N

🚗 $10-11.50, 15-20 min.

🚐 VIA limo every 30 min, 6 am-midnight. $6. To El Tropicano, St. Anthony Inter-Continental, Gunter, Hyatt Regency, Hilton, Four Seasons, Holiday Inn Downtown, Marriott. Other hotels on request.

🚌 No. 12 Airport Express M-F only. Operates to the airport from Travis & Broadway, downtown, approx every

30 min 5:40-9:20 am. Only service into city is afternoon schedule every 30 min 4:18-7:05 pm. 20-30 min ride downtown. 75¢. Bus stop at "VIA" sign next to taxi stand.

🚗 Alamo, American Intl, Avis, Budget, Dollar, Enterprise, General, Hertz, National, Payless, Snappy, Thrifty.

**P** ST $5.50, LT $3.30.

## SAN DIEGO, California
San Diego Intl Airport, 3 mi NW

🚕 $5-6, but best to confirm fare in advance with driver. Cabs are deregulated. 5-10 min downtown.

🚐 Door-to-door shared-van service to downtown, Coronado, Mission Hills, Normal Heights, Point Loma, Chula Vista, La Mesa, San Carlos, Rancho Bernardo, Escondido, La Jolla, Oceanside, El Cajon, San Ysidro. Two operators: Peerless Vans, 800-367-4093 (US), 619-481-2362; Airporter Express, 619-280-1789. Per person fares range from $4 downtown to $30 to Escondido/Oceanside. Call for exact charge and boarding info.

🚌 No. 2 bus every 20 min M-F, every 30 min Sat-Sun, 5:05 am-11:35 pm. 15-min ride to 3rd & Broadway, downtown. $1 exact fare. Catch return ride along Broadway.

🚗 Avis, Budget, General, Hertz, National.

**P** ST $8, 1-2 days; $10 each day thereafter. LT $5.

## SAN FRANCISCO, California
San Francisco Intl Airport, 14 mi S

🚕 $24 flat rate fare anywhere in the city. Up to five passengers can share a ride. Limit of three drop-offs. Nonstop downtown run is 20 min.

🚌 SFO Airporter to Meridien, Hyatt Union Square, Westin St. Francis, Hilton Nikko, Ramada Renaissance every 20 min 6:20 am-midnight. OW $4, RT $7. Board lower level outside baggage claim. **Door-to-door San Francisco** Several on-demand carriers drop off and pick up at upper level center island. $7 shared ride within city. Res: SuperShuttle 415-558-8500 or 800-554-5543 (US); Downtown Airport Express 415-775-5121; Good Neighbors AirBus 415-777-4895; Lorrie's 415-826-5950; Yellow Van Service 415-861-7291.

🚌 SamTrans buses No. 7B, 7F daily 5:43 am-1:21 am at 15-, 30-min intervals. No luggage allowed on 7F. Leave from upper level at SamTrans sign. $1.25 exact. 30-50 min ride to Transbay Terminal, 1st & Mission, downtown.

🚍 No. 3B bus from SamTrans boarding area upper level, 50¢ to Daly City BART station. Bus operates 5:52 am-6:22 pm every 30 min M-F, every 30-60 min 8:30 am-4:30 pm Sat-Sun-Hol. BART cost $1.10 addl to downtown. Scenic but no fun if you are wrestling luggage.

**To Oakland Intl Airport** Bay Area Bus Service Airporter on the hour 7 am-midnight with stops on call at Treasure Island, Oakland Army Base, Oakland Hyatt Regency. $7, 60 min. **To San Jose Municipal Airport** Greyhound at 8:40 am, 3:25 pm daily. $7, 50 min.

🚗 Alamo, Alpine, American Intl, Apple, AVCar, Avis, Budget, Dollar, General, Hertz, National, Payless, RPM, Showcase, Snappy, Thrifty, Wheels for Rent.

**P** ST $13, LT $8. Free shuttle every 5-15 min.

**To Marin County** Marin Airporter every 30 min 6 am-Midnight. Sausalito, Mill Valley $8; Larkspur $9; Terra Linda $10; Ignacio $11; Novato $12. Santa Rosa Airporter hourly 6:30 am-11:30 pm to Howard Johnson's/Shoreline Hwy $8; Corte Madera Inn $9; San Rafael Greyhound $10; Terra Linda 101 off-ramp $10; Marinwood 101 off-ramp $11; Novato Travelodge $12. Info: 707-898-8888. **Concord/Berkeley** Airport Connection to Emeryville, Durant, Claremont, Orinda, Walnut Creek, Concord. Fares $12-16. Info: (US) 800-AIRPORT, 415-363-1500. **To Travis AFB, Vallejo** Travis Express, US 800-521-4086, 707-437-4611. **To Fremont, Union City, Newark** Fun Connection every 2 hrs 7 am-10 pm. $13. 415-791-7160. **To Santa Rosa, Rohnert Park, Petaluma** Sonoma County Airport Express hourly 6 am-midnight. $8. **To Sonoma, Boyes Spring, Kenwood, Glen Ellen** Sonoma Airporter at 8:05, 9:45 am; 12:20, 2:45, 5:40 pm weekdays; 9:45 am, 12:20, 5:50 pm weekends. **To Napa, Vallejo** Evans Airport Service about every 90 min 6:30 am to 11:45 pm. Vallejo $10, Napa $11. **To Castro Valley, Dublin, San Ramon, Danville, Pleasanton, Alamo** San Ramon Airport Express about every 2 hrs 6:45 am-10:15 pm. $17. **To Emeryville, Berkeley, North Oakland** Bay Area Shuttle about every hour 6:30 am-10:35 pm. $10. **To Orinda, Walnut Creek, Concord** Bay Porter Express hourly 6:30 am-11:30 pm. $14-16.

**All suburban services board center island, lower level.**


🚌 **To Ft. Ord, Monterey, Salinas** Greyhound at 8:40, 10:55 am; 12:50, 3:25, 7:10, 9:25 pm. **To Los Gatos, Santa Cruz, Sunnyvale** Greyhound 10:55 am; 4:30, 7:10 pm. **To Sacramento** Greyhound at 8:55, 10:50, 11:55 am; 2:05, 3:55, 5, 9:50 pm. **To San Jose** Greyhound at 6:50, 8:40 am; 12:50, 3:25, 7:10, 9:25 pm. Purchase ticket at insurance desk, central terminal. Greyhound info: 415-877-0366.

# SAN JOSE, California
San Jose Intl Airport, 3 mi NW

🚕 $7-8, 7-10 min. Same fare and travel time to bus, RR stations. To Santa Clara, $7.50; Sunnyvale, $9-12; Cupertino, $16-18; Palo Alto, $20-25.

🚐 No scheduled service to San Jose. **To Santa Cruz** Peerless Stages has 7 departures 8:40 am-8:35 pm. Intermediate stops at Los Gatos, Scotts Valley. $4.05 to Santa Cruz. **To Sunnyvale, Palo Alto, Stanford, Menlo Park, and other towns in the area** BayPorter Express, 800-548-8811.

🚌 Santa Clara County Transit No. 64 from bus shelter outside baggage claim. For downtown, take No. 64 Almaden Valley. Departures every 15 min 6 am-12:07 am. 75¢. 15-20 min downtown. **To Fremont, Milpitas** Transfer at Hedding & Fourth to No. 180 bus. 75¢ ($1 express) fare to driver. **To Monterey** Greyhound at 9:40 am; 5, 8:05, 10:20 pm. **To San Francisco Intl Airport (SFO)** BayPorter Express. $16. Reservation required: 800-548-8811.

🚗 Alamo, Avis, Budget, Dollar, General, Hertz, National, Pacific USA, Payless, Thrifty.

**P** ST $24, LT $6. Shuttle every 5 min to LT lot.

# SAN JOSE, Costa Rica
Juan Santamaria Airport, 10 mi (16 km) NW

🚕 C600 ($7.50), 20 min. To Puntarenas, $44, 1 hr; to Limon, $94, 1 hr 45 min; to San Carlos, $31; to San Isidro del General, $75, 2 hrs. Cabs are orange colored. No tips.

🚐 Microbus for 5+ persons, C800 ($10) total to San Jose.

🚌 Alajuela-San Jose bus every 20 min 4 am-11 pm from stop across street from airport. Fare C24 (30¢). Baggage OK.

🚕 Ada, Budget, Dollar, Hertz, Toyota.

**P** C450 ($5.60)/day.

## SAN JUAN, Puerto Rico
Puerto Rico Intl Airport, 5 mi E

🚕 $10, 15 min.

🚌 $2.50, 20 min.

🚕 Avis, Budget, Hertz, National, Thrifty.

## SAN PEDRO SULA, Honduras
LaMesa Airport, 9 mi (15 km) E

🚕 £15 ($5.40), 15 min. Haggling over price not uncommon. A good bargainer may get the price down to £10 ($3.60).

🚕 Blitz, Budget, Molinari.

## SAN SALVADOR, El Salvador
El Salvador Intl Airport, 30 mi (48 km) SE

🚕 CO80 ($16), 25 min to city center, hotels. Tip 10%.

🚌 ACACYA coach at 11 am, 5, 7 pm daily. CO15 ($5), 30 min.

🚕 Avis, Budget, Hertz, Imosa, Superior.

**P** CO9 ($1.80)/day.

## SANTA BARBARA, California
Santa Barbara Municipal Airport, 6 mi W

🚗 $16, 20 min.

🚗 Avis, Budget, Dollar, Hertz, National, Thrifty.

## SANTA FE, New Mexico
Santa Fe Municipal Airport, 9 mi SW

🚗 $13 flat fare plus tax, $1 per person for more than 3. 15-20 min.

🚌 **To/from Albuquerque** Shuttlejack Coach from Inn at Loretto and Hilton Inn (5 min later) to Albuquerque at 5, 7, 9, 9:45. 11 am; 1:15, 1:55, 3:30, 5:15, 8:30 pm. From Albuquerque at 6:55, 8:55, 11:10, 11:40 am; 2, 3:25, 5:10, 6:45, 8:15, 10:15 pm. 75-min trip. $15 OW. Res: 505-982-4311.

🚗 Avis, Budget, Hertz, National.

## SANTIAGO, Chile
Santiago Intl Airport, 10 mi (16 km)

🚗 $10-12, 30 min to city center. No tip.

🚌 Every 30 min 6:30 am-9 pm to Moneda 1523, city center. Fare 90¢. 30-min ride. Look for bus in front of airport.

🚗 Atal, Avis, Budget, Chilean, Dollar, Hertz, National, Rentauto

## SANTO DOMINGO, Dominican Republic
Aeropuerto Intl de las Americas, 17 mi (27 km) W

🚗 DRP$35 ($13), 25 min. No tip necessary.

🚗 Avis, Budget, Cima, Cumbre, Dollar, Express, Hertz, Nelly, Patsy, Puerto Rico.

## SAO PAULO, Brazil
Congonhas Airport, 9 mi (14.4km) SW

🚕 Red/white cabs. Cr2100 ($6), 15 min. Tip 10%. Note that three types of cabs are available: Small cabs, often Volkswagens, carry two people and a few pieces of baggage. Fare Cr1400 ($4). Next are standard-size cars, like the red/white listed here. Deluxe cabs, A/C, are the largest and most expensive. Fare Cr2800 ($8). Look for cab dispatcher.

🚌 Bus to city center every 5 min on Ave. Washington Luis, in front of airport. Cr50 (15¢), 35-40 min. No room for baggage, often crowded and uncomfortable. **To Sao Paulo Intl Airport (Guarulhos)** Metro bus every 30-45 min 5:45 am-9:25 pm. Cr120 ($2).

🚗 Avis, Hertz, Interlocadora, Localiza, Locarauto, Unidas.
**P** Cr2000 ($5.70)/day.

## SAO PAULO, Brazil
Sao Paulo Intl Airport (Guarulhos), 18 mi (30km) NE

🚕 Blue/white Radio Taxis. Cr1860 ($11), 25-30 min to Republica Sq. Tip 10%. If taxi is unmetered, take care to confirm fare with driver.

🚌 Metro bus every 30 min 6 am-1 am, then hourly on the hour. Cr700 ($2). Purchase ticket in advance on ground floor in national arrivals section. 35-40 min to Praca de Republica (Republic Sq). **To Congonhas Airport for Rio shuttle, domestic flights** Metro bus every 30-45 min 7:15 am-9:25 pm. Cr800 ($2.30).

🚗 Avis, Hertz, Interlocadora, Localiza, Locarauto, Unidas.
**P** Cr390 ($1.50)/day.

## SAO PAULO, Brazil
Viracopos Airport, 56 mi (90 km) W

🚗 Cr15600 ($44.60), 90 min. To Sao Paulo Intl Airport (Guarulhos), Cr 18250 ($52), 80-100 min. Tip 10%. Because of the distance to Sao Paulo, taxis are very expensive and not in great demand. They are not metered and one must come to an arrangement with the driver as to a fare. He can charge round-trip rate for a one-way ride. Best to agree in advance what the fare will be.

🚌 Airlines provide free transport between this charter-flight airport and the city. Inquire.

🚗 Columbia, Hertz, Interlocadora, Localiza.

P Cr500 ($1.40)/day.

## SARASOTA/BRADENTON, Florida
Sarasota-Bradenton Airport, 6 mi N of Sarasota

🚗 $8, 15 min to Sarasota; $14, 25 min to Bradenton.

🚗 Ajax, Alamo, American Intl, Avis, Budget, Dollar, Enterprise, Hertz, National, Payless, Snappy, Thrifty.

P ST $7.50, LT $4.

## SASKATOON, Saskatchewan
Saskatoon Airport, 4.5 mi NW

🚗 C$7.50 ($5.70), 15-20 min. Tip 10%.

🚗 Avis, Budget, Hertz, Thrifty, Tilden.

## SAVANNAH, Georgia
Savannah Municipal Airport, 8 mi NW

🚗 $15 flat fare, $3 each addl passenger. 15-20 min.

🚗 Alamo, Avis, Budget, Dollar, Enterprise, Hertz, National, Snappy, Thrifty.

# SEATTLE/TACOMA, Washington

Seattle-Tacoma Intl Airport, 13 mi S of Seattle, 23 mi N of Tacoma

🚐 Seattle center, $20.50-28.50, 20-40 min; ferry dock, $21-23; hotels, $21-26; university, $26-30; Renton $10-12.50; Bellevue $23.50-28.50; Kirkland, $25-35; Federal Way, $14-18; Tacoma, $28.50-37, 30-45 min.

🚌 Gray Line Airport Express to downtown Seattle every 15-30 min 5:30 am -midnight. $5 OW, $9 RT. Purchase ticket at booth curbside. 25-50 min. Stops at Stouffer Madison, Crowne Plaza, Four Seasons Olympic, Hilton, Sheraton, Westin, Warwick, Best Western Executive Inn. Not all stops each run. Ask agent. Info: 206-626-6088. **To Tacoma** Travelines Airporter hourly 5:50 am-10:55 pm Sun-Fri, every 2 hrs Sat, Hol. Also stops at Federal Way, Fife. $8-10, pay driver. 40-45 min to LaQuinta, Sheraton; Tacoma Dome by res. **To Bellingham** Airporter 8, 11 am; 1, 3, 6 pm. $20 OW,$36 RT. **To Vancouver, B.C.** Quick Coach. 12:30 3, 10 pm; $32. **To Everett, Lynwood** Everett Airporter hourly 6:30 am-11:45 pm, $7-11. **To Ft. Lewis & McChord AFB** Ft. Lewis/McChord Airporter at 7 am then every 2 hrs to 11 pm. $7-8 **To Bellevue & N of Lake Washington** Suburban Airporter every 30-60 min 5:50 am-12:30 am. 25 min, $7.50 to Bellevue.

🚌 No. 174 bus every 30 min 5:21 am-12:20 am, Sat from 6:17 am, Sun from 7:05 am and hourly until 10:05 am then every 30 min until 12:20 am. No. 194 M-F express every 30 min 8:29 am-6:20 pm. $1. Buses depart S end of baggage claim. Look for Metro sign. 45-50 min run to 4th Ave. & Union St. downtown. Express run, 27 min. **To Renton, Bellevue, Aurora Village** No. 340 bus about every 30 min 6:01 am-9:15 pm. Hourly 8:22 am-9:22 pm Sat, Sun. **To Tacoma** No. 174 bus southbound. Transfer at Federal Way to Pierce No. 500 for downtown Tacoma.

🚗 Alamo, Avis, Budget, Dollar, Hertz, Mini-Rate, National, Pacific, Payless, Rent-A-Wreck, Thrifty.

**P** First 30 min free. $10/day. No LT lot on airport grounds but private lots available; free transportation.

## SEOUL, Korea
Kimpo Intl Airport, 11.5 mi (19km) W

🚗 Regular cabs are painted blue, yellow, green, or orange. OK for 3 adults plus bags. For 4-5 passengers, a gold-colored "Call" cab required. Call fares are double regular fares. Sample regular fares: Hyatt Regency, 26 km, W3600 ($5); Seoul Hilton, 20 km, W2850 ($4); Olympic Sports Complex, 34 km, W4700 ($6.50). Rates posted at loading zone. No tip.

🚌 Two routes, same fare of W500 (70¢) and 10-min frequency on each. **No. 600** To Sports Complex, Jamsil via Heuk Suk Dong, Seoul Palace Hotel, Express Bus Terminal, Riverside Hotel, Youngs-dong, Nan Seoul Hotel, Aid Apt, Koex. **No.601** To Sheraton Walker Hill Hotel via City Hall Plaza hotels: President, Lotte, Seoul Plaza, Westin Chosun. About 30-, 40-min ride to town. Ample baggage space, very comfortable. Boards at center, arrivals hall.

🚌 Three express bus routes, OK for commuters with light or no luggage. No. 63 to City Hall. No. 68 to railway station, City Hall area. No. 700 to Yongdungpo-Yoido. Departures every 10 min 6 am-10 pm. Fare W350 (50¢). Bus presently picks up to left outside arrival hall. But note that completion of new intl terminal for Olympics may change location.

🚗 Hertz, Korean Express Co.

**P** W4900 ($6.80)/day.

**Note:** Seoul subway, though it does not connect to airport, is fast, clean, safe, well marked in English, and very inexpensive. Good bet for local transportation.

## SHANGHAI, China
Hongqiao Airport, 9.3 mi (15 km) W

🚕 RY15.60 ($4.40), 25 min. No tip.

🚌 CAAC provides transfer from airport to city ticket office. RY1.8 (50¢), 30 min.

🚗 Self-drive cars not available in China, but chauffeur-driven are. Inquire at hotel.

## SHANNON, Ireland
Shannon Intl Airport, 15 mi (24 km) NW of Limerick

🚕 £14 ($20), 30 min into town. Tip 10%.

🚌 Bus Eireann to Limerick RR station about every 30 min from 7:55 am, less frequent Sat. Sun service about every 90 min from 8 am. Last evening bus 10:10 pm; final service at 12:05 am. Baggage room. Pay £2.60 ($4.20) fare aboard. About 45-min ride.

🚗 Avis, Budget, Hertz, Johnson & Perrott, Murray's, Europcar.

## SHREVEPORT, Louisiana
Shreveport Regional Airport, 5 mi SW

🚕 $8.25, 15 min.

🚗 Avis, Budget, Hertz, National, Thrifty.

# SINGAPORE
Changi Airport, 12.5 mi (20 km) NE

🚗 S$13 ($6.40) including airport surcharge, 25 min. Add S$1 (50¢) for luggage placed in trunk. Add S50¢ (25¢) each for third, fourth rider. Surcharge midnight-6 am, 50% of metered fare.

🚌 No. 390 from Basement 2 of terminal every 15-20 min 6 am-11:45 pm. Pay driver S80¢ (40¢) exact change. No baggage racks. 40-50 min to city center. Clean and reasonably comfortable.

🚗 Avis, Sintat.

**P** ST S$15 ($7.40), LT S$8 ($3.90).

# SIOUX FALLS, South Dakota
Joe Foss Field, 3 mi N

🚗 $4.50, 10 min.

🚗 Avis, Budget, Dollar, Hertz, National.

# SOUTHEND, England
Southend Airport, 2 mi (3.2 km) N of Southend, 35 mi (56 km) E of London

🚗 £2 ($3.50) to Southend, 10 min. Cab to London—£35 ($60), 60-90 min—not recommended.

🚆 Bus or taxi to Rochford Station, 6 min. Then British Rail connection to London Fenchurch Station. Departures approx half-hourly, 58-min ride. £6.20 ($10.60).

🚗 Godfrey Davis/Europcar.

# SPARTANBURG, South Carolina
See GREENVILLE/SPARTANBURG, South Carolina.

## SPOKANE, Washington
Spokane Intl Airport, 6 mi SW

🚗 $12, addl passengers 50¢ each. 15-20 min.

🚗 Avis, Budget, Dollar, Hertz, National, Payless, Thrifty.

## SPRINGFIELD, Illinois
Capital Airport, 3 mi N

🚗 To state office complex, one person, $5; two or more, $4 each. 10-15 min. To Holiday Inn East Conference Center, $8 per person, 20 min. To Sangamon State U., $10 per person, 25-30 min.

🚗 Avis, Budget, Hertz, National.

## SPRINGFIELD, Massachusetts
See HARTFORD, Connecticut/SPRINGFIELD, Massachusetts.

## SPRINGFIELD, Missouri
Springfield Regional Airport, 8 mi NW

🚗 $7.65, addl passengers 50¢ each. 15 min.

🚗 Avis, Budget, Hertz, National.

## ST. CROIX, Virgin Islands
Alexander Hamilton Airport, 7.5 mi SW

🚗 $4 flat rate per person, 20 min to Christiansted; to Frederiksted, $4 per person, 20 min; to Queens Quarter Hotel, $4 per person, 10 min. Baggage: first piece free, second 30¢. 40¢ for trunk.

🚗 Avis, Budget, Discount, Dollar, Hertz, National, Playboy, Thrifty.

## ST. LOUIS, Missouri
Lambert St. Louis Intl Airport, 13 mi NW

🚕 $16-17 downtown, 20-30 min. Addl passengers 50¢ each. To Clayton $12-13.

🚐 Jet Port van every 20 min 6:30 am-10:30 pm. $6 OW, $11 RT to downtown, midtown, Clayton hotels. Info: 314-427-8119.

🚌 No. 104X express inbound M-F only at 6:24, 6:42, 7:01, 8:02 am. Outbound at 4:41, 5:03, 5:20, 5:48 pm. $1 exact. 55-min run. Info: 314-231-2345.

🚗 Avis, Budget, Dollar, Hertz, National.

**P** ST $8, LT $4.

## ST. LUCIA, West Indies
Hewanorra Intl Airport, 33 mi SE of Castries; Vigie Field, 2 mi N of Castries

🚕 From Hewanorra $30, 60 min. From Vigie $4, 5 min. Vigie to Cariblue Hotel $10; St. Lucian $8; Halcyon Beach $4.

🚗 Avis, National.

## ST. MAARTEN, Netherlands Antilles
Princess Juliana Intl Airport, 7 mi W

🚕 To Philipsburg, Naf12.60 ($7) for 1-2 passengers, $1 each addl. 20 min. To Marigot (French capital), $7, 15 min; to Mullet Bay Hotel, $4, 7 min; to La Samana Hotel, $8, 15 min.

🚗 Avis, Beach Island, Budget, Cannegie, Caribbean, Diamond, Dollar, Hertz, Holiday, National, Opel, Reggie's, Risdon, Roy Rogers, Speedy, Sunshine.

**P** 50¢/hour.

## ST. PAUL, Minnesota
See MINNEAPOLIS/ST. PAUL, Minnesota.

## ST. THOMAS, Virgin Islands
Cyril E. King Airport, 3 mi W

🚗 $3 flat rate per person, 10 min to Charlotte Amalie.

🚘 Avis, Budget, Hertz, National, Olympic.

## STOCKHOLM, Sweden
Arlanda Airport, 26.25 mi (42 km) N

🚗 SKr 250-300 ($38.50-46.20), 35-40 min. Tip 10%. A less costly weekday alternative between 8 am and 4 pm: look for "Arlanda Retur" car. Fare Skr 150 ($23).

🚐 SAS car (may be shared ride): SKr 185-275 ($28.50-42.35) per person into city. Return car must be ordered at least 4 hrs in advance, phone 797-3700.

🚌 Arlanda Airport (SL) bus to Central Station (Vasagatan), Stockholm City. 7:10 am-10:30 pm at 10-,20-min intervals; thereafter meets flights. SKr30 ($4.60). Pay driver or purchase ticket in advance at airport or city terminals. Baggage racks. 40-45 min. All buses stop on north side of Stockholm at Haga Park Air Terminal and Ulriksdal Air Terminal. Central Station is at Vasagatan 6-14. To Brommaplan, Sundbybergs Torg, Kista Centrum: Departures every 30-60 min 6:20 am-11 pm. **To Uppsala** Bus No. 801 every 30 min 5:50 am-12:20 am. SKr22 ($3.40). 40-min journey.

🚘 Avis, Budget, Europcar, Hertz, InterRent.

**P** SKr 35 ($5.50)/day.

## STUTTGART, West Germany
Stuttgart/Echterdingen Airport, 9 mi (14 km) S

🚕 DM30 ($16.25), 15-20 min into town. Stuttgart is birthplace of the Mercedes Benz and there are plenty of them waiting at the cab stand.

🚌 SSB Express bus at 6:25, 7:25 am, then every 20-40 min to 11:35 pm. Baggage room, comfortable seats. 20 min to Central Air Terminal and Hauptbahnhof. Fare DM6 ($3.25).

🚗 Autohansa, Avis, Europcar, Hertz, InterRent, Mages, Scheer, Sixt-Budget.

**P** ST DM30 ($16.25), LT DM5 ($2.70).

## SUN VALLEY, Idaho
Friedman Memorial Airport, 11 mi S

🚕 $10 per passenger, 20 min.

🚐 Elkhorn Lodge operates courtesy limo for registered guests.

🚗 Avis, Budget, Federal, Hertz, National.

**P** $2/day.

## SURFERS PARADISE, Australia
Coolangatta Airport, 15.5 mi (25 km) S

🚕 A$16 ($12.80), 30 min.

🚐 EET coaches meet flights. A$5 ($4), 30-45 min to major hotels on the Gold Coast. Buy ticket in terminal.

🚗 Avis, Budget, Hertz, Thrifty.

**P** A$8 ($6.40)/day.

## SYDNEY, Australia
Kingsford Smith Airport, 6.2 mi (10 km) S

🚕 A$15 ($12), 20-40 min to Regent Hotel, city center.

🚌 No. 300 Airport Express every 20-30 min 6:25 am-10:15 pm from intl terminal, stopping at domestic terminal, then to Central Station and Circular Quay downtown, near hotels. A$3 ($2.40).

🚌 Kingsford Smith Transport bus to all major hotels in city and King's Cross every 30 min 6 am-8 pm. To city A$3.80 ($3).

**To Wollongong** Watts Bus Service, A$11 ($8.80).

🚗 Avis, Budget, Commonwealth, Hertz, Thrifty.

**P** ST A$9 ($7.20), LT A$4 ($3.20).

## SYRACUSE, New York
Hancock Intl Airport, 6.5 mi NE

🚕 $10.50. 10-15 min.

🚗 Ajax, American Intl, Avis, Budget, Dollar, Hertz, National, Snappy, Thrifty.

## TACOMA, Washington
See SEATTLE/TACOMA, Washington.

## TAIPEI, Taiwan
Chiang Kai-Shek Intl Airport, 25 mi (40 km) S

🚕 T$800 ($24). 40-50 min. No tip required.

🚌 Taiwan Motor Transport Co. every 15-30 min. Pay T$72 ($2.15) fare before boarding. Two routes: one to Miramar Hotel, Taipei Airport; other to Ambassador Hotel, Taipei train station, Lai Lai Shangrila Hotel, Chung Luen bus station. First bus 7:05 am, last 11:30 pm. 45-60 min ride.

🚗 Hertz.

**P** T$80 ($2.60)/day.

## TALLAHASSEE, Florida
Tallahassee Municipal Airport, 8 mi SW

🚗 $10.60, addl riders 50¢ each. 15-20 min.

🚘 Avis, Budget, Dollar, Hertz, National.


## TAMPA-ST. PETERSBURG, Florida
Tampa Intl Airport, 5 mi NW of Tampa; 15 mi NE of St. Petersburg

🚗 **To Tampa** $12-15, addl riders 25¢ each, 10-15 min.
**To St. Petersburg**
$34 flat rate, 30-35 min.

🚐 **To Tampa** Central Florida Limousine, $9. Service at all times. **To St. Petersburg** The Limo, $10. Meets all flights.

🚌 **To Tampa** No. 30 Downtown bus from red departure level every 35-40 min 6:08 am-7:58 pm M-F; hourly 6:45 am-7:35 pm Sat, 9:58 am-5:40 pm Sun. 60¢. 30-min ride downtown. **To St. Pete/Clearwater Airport** The Limo, $10. Meets all incoming flights. Info: 813-572-1111.

🚘 Ajax, Alamo, American Intl, Avis, Budget, Dollar, Enterprise, General, Hertz, National, Payless, Snappy, Thrifty.

**P** ST $7, LT $5.


## TAMPICO, Mexico
Gen. F. Javier Mina Airport, 5 mi (8 km) NW

🚗 $3, 15-20 min.

🚘 Avis, Hertz.

# TEESIDE, England

Teeside Intl Airport, 6 mi E of Darlington, 13 mi W of Middlesborough

🚗 £3.50 ($6) to Darlington, 12 min; £6.50 ($11.15) to Middlesborough, 25 min.

🚆 Local diesel every 30-60 min. To Darlington, 14 min; Middlesborough, 20 min.

🚌 To Darlington £1.20 ($2.05), 20 min.

🚘 Avis, Hertz, Godfrey Davis/Europcar.


# TEGUCIGALPA, Honduras

Toncontin Airport, 5 mi (8 km) SE

🚗 To Prado, Plaza, Honduras Maya hotels, £15 ($5.40), 15-20 min.

🚘 Blitz, Budget, Molinari.


# TEL AVIV, Israel

Ben Gurion Intl Airport, 12.5 mi (20 km) E

🚗 Two types. Sherut: Mercedes that carry up to 7 persons, $4 each. 24-hr service. 15-20 min. Sherut to Jerusalem, $7 per person. Private taxis: $11.25 to Tel Aviv. After 9 pm 25% addl. Baggage over 4 pcs, 30¢ each. Tip 10-15%. Fares set by Ministry of Tourism—look for posted rates. It's easier to pay in US dollars than Israeli shekels.

🚍 United Tours bus hourly on the hour. $1.50, 20-30 min. Serves Dan, Sheraton, Ramada, Diplomat, Hilton, Plaza, Carlton hotels, RR station. A/C.

🚌 Natl Israel Bus (EGGED) bus every 15 min 5:30 am-11 pm. 35-40 min to Central Bus Station. $1.05 to driver. Usually A/C. Comfortable but not much baggage room. To Jerusalem, $2.50. Note that last bus on Shabbat (Friday) is at 3 pm.

🚗 Avis, Budget, Eldan, Europcar, Hansa Intl, Hertz, InterRent.

**P** $2/day.

## TENERIFE, Canary Islands
Reina-Sofia Airport, 37 mi (60 km) SW of Santa Cruz de Tenerife

🚕 Taxis available for hire to any part of island. Trip time to Santa Cruz 60 min. Determine fare in advance.

🚗 Avis, Cicar, Intercanarias, Nuevos Destinos, Suncars.

## TIJUANA, Mexico
Gen. Abelardo Rodriguez Airport, 10 mi (16 km) NE

🚕 $7, 15-20 min.

🚗 Alliance, Avis, Budget, Hertz, National.

## TOKYO, Japan
Haneda Airport, 18 mi (29 km) S

🚕 Y5400 ($40), tip not required. 35-40 min to city center.

🚆 Monorail, about $1.80. Service every 7 min 7 am-11 pm. 15 min to Hamamatsu-Cho. Taxi from city station.

🚗 Avis, Budget, Hertz, Toyota.

# TOKYO, Japan

New Tokyo Intl (Narita) Airport, 42 mi (67 km) W

🚗 Y20,000 ($150) including tolls, tip not required. 60-90 min downtown.

🚌 Airport Limousine Bus every 5 min peak times, up to 20 min other times. Purchase ticket, Y2500 ($18.75), before boarding. Service from 6:50 am-midnight. Travel time 70 min to Tokyo City Air Terminal at Hakozaki-Cho. From there it's a cab ride to hotel or business.

🚌 Airport Limousine Bus or Shuttle to downtown hotels. Fares range Y2600-2700 ($19.50-20.25). Buy ticket before boarding. Departures at least hourly. Travel time 70 min in normal traffic, longer in rush periods. Direct service to hotels in Ikebukuro, Shinjuku, Akasaka, Ginza, Shiba, Shinagawa, Haneda areas.

🚊 6-min shuttle bus to Keisei Line Narita Station. Shuttle Y190 ($1.40). Choice from Keisei Station: Skyliner Express, 60 min, Y1510 ($11.35); or Limited Express, 75 min, Y810 ($6.10). Both terminate Keisei Ueno Station. Purchase tickets at airport counter. Train service every 30 min. Comfortable, baggage space. Plenty of cabs available in city.

🚌 **To Japan Railway (JR) Tokyo Station** JR Shuttle from airport to JR Narita Stn. Y370 ($2.70), 25 min. Choice of trains at station: JR Rapid, 80 min, Y1060 ($8); JR Limited Express "Ayame," 60 min, Y2460 ($18.45). **To Haneda Airport** Limo every 30 min. Y2700 ($20). 1 hr 40 min. **To Yokohama City Air Terminal** Limo every 30-60 min. Y3100 ($23) 2 hrs.

🚗 Avis, Budget, Hertz, Toyota.

# TOLEDO, Ohio
Toledo Express Airport, 17 mi SW

🚗 $28, 20 min by expressway.

🚐 Airport van, $15 first passenger, $5 each addl. 30-min run. AMEX, MC, VISA.

🚙 Avis, Budget, Hertz, National, Snappy.

# TOPEKA, Kansas
Forbes Field Airport, 7 mi S

🚗 $10.80, 15 min.

🚙 Avis, Budget, Hertz, National.

# TORONTO, Ontario
Lester B. Pearson Intl Airport, 18 mi (28 km) NW

🚗 C$24 ($19.70), 30-45 min. To Mississauga C$18 ($14.75), 20 min. Stops en route, $3. Tip 10-15%. **Questions? Look for Ground Transportation/Transport de Surface desk, lower level.**

🚐 Airport Express Gray Coach every 20 min 6:50 am-12:10 am. Buy ticket in advance at airport or hotel. Fare C$8 ($6.50) OW, C$13.50 ($10.95) RT. 20-35 min to Harbour Castle Westin, Royal York, L'Hotel (Convention Centre), Sheraton Centre (Hilton Intl), Holiday Inn (Bus Terminal), Delta Chelsea Inn.

🚊 Airport Express Gray Coach to Islington subway station. Departures every 30-40 min 7 am-12:40. Buy coach ticket in advance, C$4.25 ($2.80) OW, C$7 ($5.65) RT. Subway fare C$1.05 OW, C$2 RT ($1.60). Toronto subway is clean, easy to navigate with luggage. 20-min ride to Yonge & Bloor, downtown.

🚙 Avis, Budget, Hertz, Thrifty, Tilden, Travellers.

**P** ST C$10 ($7), LT C$7.50 ($6.15). **To Woodstock, London, Strathroy, Sarnia** Robert Q's Airbus at 1-2 hr intervals 8 am-12:30 am. Info, res: 519-673-6804. **To Woodstock, London** Aboutown Transit London every 2-3 hours 8:30 am-12:30 am. 519-663-2222.

## TORTOLA, British Virgin Islands
Beef Island Airport, 8 mi (13 km) E

🚕 $4 per person, 30 min. Tip $1.

🚗 Anytime, Avis, Budget, Speedy's.

## TRAVERSE CITY, Michigan
Cherry Capital Airport, 3 mi SE

🚕 $4.50, 10 min.

🚗 Avis, Budget, Hertz, National, Thrifty.

**P** $2/day first 5 days, $1/day thereafter.

## TRINIDAD/TOBAGO
Piarco Intl Airport, 16 mi (25 km) SE of Port of Spain

🚕 TT$50 ($14), 35 min to Port of Spain. To San Fernando, TT$90 ($25), 45 min; to Arima, TT$30 ($8.50), 15 min. Tip discretionary but TT$5 ($1.50) minimum acceptable.

🚌 Public Transit Service Corp bus from front of terminal every 30 min 5 am-11 pm. TT$1.50 (40¢), 30 min to Port of Spain. No baggage.

🚗 Auto Rentals Limited, Singhs

**P** TT$25 ($7)/day.

## TUCSON, Arizona
Tucson Intl Airport, 10 mi S

🚕 Taxi fares deregulated—confirm with driver. Yellow offers best rate downtown, $12-15, but must be called: 602-624-6611. 15-20 min ride.

🚐 Arizona Stagecoach Airport Limousine, $8 to downtown hotel. To private residence in central area, $9 first person, $5 each addl same address.

🚌 No. 8 every 30-60 min 5:33 am-7:15 pm M-F, less frequent Sat-Sun schedule. 60¢ exact. 35 min to Church & Broadway.

🚗 Ajax, Alamo, American Intl, Avis, Budget, Dollar, Enterprise, Hertz, National, Snappy, Thrifty.

## TULSA, Oklahoma
Tulsa Intl Airport, 9 mi NE

🚗 $10, addl passengers 75¢ each. 15-20 min.

🚗 Avis, Budget, Dollar, Enterprise, Hertz, National, Snappy, Thrifty.

## VAIL, Colorado
Avon Stolport, 8 mi W

🚕 $14.35, 15 min, to Mid Vail; To Beaver Creek Resort, $5.25, 5 min; to East Vail, $21, 20 min. Each addl ride $1, plus 50¢ airport head tax.

🚐 Colorado Mtn Express shuttle meets flights 7 am-9 pm. To Vail, $6, 15 min. To Beaver Creek Resort, $3.50, 5 min. To East Vail, $8, 20 min.**See also Denver listing for Resort Express service to Vail, Beaver Creek.**

🚗 Budget, Hertz.

**P** Free.

## VALLETTA, Malta

Luqa Airport, 4 mi (6 km) SW

🚖 Always available, 15 min.

🚌 No. 32, 34, 35 bus every 20 min 6 am-10 pm.

🚗 Avis, Hertz.

P Free.

## VANCOUVER, British Columbia

Vancouver Intl Airport, 11 mi SW

🚖 C$15 ($11.25), 23-30 min.

🚐 Perimeter Transportation, C$6.25 ($4.70) to downtown hotels. 20-30 min.

🚗 Avis, Budget, Dollar, Hertz, Thrifty, Tilden.

P ST C$7 ($5.25), LT C$3.50 ($2.65).

## VENICE, Italy

Marco Polo Airport, 8 mi (13 km) NE

🚖 Lit16,000 ($12), 15 min to Piazzale Roma, where one transfers to a vaporetto mini-ferry or a water taxi. Tip landside driver 5-10%. **Water taxi** Lit60,000 ($45) for door-to-door service. One fare covers up to 8 people.

**Water bus** Lit9000 ($6.75) per person. Set route includes Rialto, Piazza San Marco, some major hotels. About 45 min.

🚌 ATVO bus coincides with flight schedule. Buy ticket for Lit2500 ($1.85) at ATVO counter in airport. Plenty of baggage space. 20 min to Piazzale Roma.

**Water bus** Express, Lit1500 ($1.10). Tickets must be purchased and validated before boarding. Any suitcase larger than a briefcase requires a ticket. A 24-hour ticket good for unlimited use costs Lit8000 ($6) and entitles bearer to carry one small suitcase aboard free.

🚗 Autorent, Avis, Europcar, Hertz, InterRent, Italy by Car/Budget, Maggiore.

## VERACRUZ, Mexico
Gen. Heriberto Jara Airport, 5 mi (8 km) SW

🚗 $4, 15 min.

🚐 5-passenger colectivos available for less than cab.

🚗 Avis, Budget, Dollar, Hertz.

## VIENNA, Austria
Schwechat Airport, 10 mi (16 km) SE

🚗 S320 approx. ($24.65), 20-30 min. Bags S10-20 (80¢-$1.60) each depending on weight.

🚐 Vienna Airport Service 7:20, 7:50 am then every 20 min to 7:10 pm. Baggage carried. 20-30 min to City Air Terminal (Hilton). Pay S50 fare ($3.85) when boarding. Return buses marked "Flughafen."

🚌 Hourly service 7 am-6 pm, 7:15 pm, to Wien Sudbahnhof (south RR station) and Wien Westbahnhof (west station); buses so marked. Baggage racks. Board directly outside terminal. Pay S50 ($3.85) to driver. 20-35 min trip.

🚆 First train 5:31 am M-Sat, 6:38 am Sun. Last train 9:03 pm (8:03 pm Sat). Frequent morning service then hourly from 8:03 am. Comfortable, good baggage racks. 30-min trip. Buy ticket for S24 ($1.85) before boarding.

🚌 Avis, Budget-Leihwagen Union, Denzel, Europcar, Hertz, Intercity, InterRent.

**P** ST S110 ($8.50), LT S68 ($5.25).

## WACO, Texas
Waco Municipal Airport, 7 mi NW

🚕 Cabs do not wait at airport, must be called. 12 min downtown, 15 min to Baylor area. Fares $5.50-6.

🚌 Avis, Hertz, National.

## WARSAW, Poland
Okecie Airport, 6 mi (10 km) SW

🚕 Zl1000-1500 ($2-4), 15 min. Tip 10%. Cabs not always easy to find. Phone number in Warsaw for radio taxi: 919.

🚐 Every 30 min 5 am-11 pm to LOT office at Warynskiego 9. Fare Zl100 (6¢).

🚌 No. 175 every 10 min 5 am-10:50 pm. Overnight service on No. 611 every 30 min 11:17 pm-4:47 am. Buy ticket for Z48 (4¢) at RUCH kiosk in departures hall, across street from arrivals hall.

🚌 Orbis Rent a Car, in arrivals hall and Forum Hotel, handles bookings for Avis, Europcar, Hertz, National.

## WASHINGTON, D.C. (Dulles)
Dulles Intl Airport, 26 mi W of Washington, DC

🚕 $32-35 to midtown DC, 45-60 min. Leesburg $19; Reston $11; Rockville $32; Bethesda NIH $31; Capitol Hill, National Airport $35; Pentagon $32.

🚌 Washington Flyer to Washington Hilton, Capital Hilton hotels at :15 and :45, 5:15 am-12:45 am, $12 OW, $20 RT. Frequent service to hotels in Bethesda/Chevy Chase, Silver Spring/Wheaton, Capital Hill, W End 22nd St. DC, Gaithersburg, Rosslyn. Info: 703-685-1400.

🚇 Washington Flyer to West Falls Church Metro Station every 45 min 6 am-10 pm M-F, Sat from 8:15 am; Sun from 10:15 am. Last Sun departure at 5 pm. 17-min ride. Transfer to Orange Line Metro. $1.65, 20-25 min to DC downtown stations. **Dulles to National Airport** Washington Flyer hourly 6 am-10 pm, also 10:30, 11:30 pm. $12 OW, $20 RT. 45 min. **To BWI** Washington Flyer shuttle every 30 min; transfer at 16th & K to BWI van. Total fare $20. 2-hr ride.

🚗 Avis, Budget, Dollar, Hertz, National.

**P** ST $26, LT $6, Satellite $4.

## WASHINGTON, D.C.
Washington National Airport, 4 mi S

🚕 Capitol area $7; business area NW, Washington Hilton $8-9; far NW addresses $10-13. DC cabs do not have meters. Fare based on distance traveled by zones. To avoid surprises, confirm in advance with driver. Virginia, Maryland cabs metered: Pentagon, $6; Rosslyn, Alexandria $7; McLean, $15; Tysons, $18; Dulles Airport, $36; BWI, $45; Baltimore downtown, $50.

🚌 Washington Flyer every 30 min 5:30 am-10:30 pm to Washington Hilton, Sheraton, Shoreham, Mayflower, Capital Hilton, Marriott. $5 OW, $9 RT. 20 min. Also serves Tysons Corner, Arlington, Reston, Silver Spring, Wheaton, Bethesda, Chevy Chase. Info: 703-685-1400.

🚐 Share-a-Limo door-to-door operated by Washington Flyer. Zone 1 (Crystal City, Capitol Hill, Downtown DC, Rosslyn, Georgetown) $7.50/person shared, $12 solo. Zone II, outside Zone I but within Beltway $12/person shared, $20 solo. Gaithersburg, Rockville shared-ride only, $15/person. Inquire at Flyer office, Main Terminal or call 703-685-1400.

🚊 Metro 6 am-midnight M-F; 8 am-midnight Sat; 10 am-midnight Sun. Station opposite N Terminal. There's a shuttle bus but it's faster to walk: 5-6 min. Buy ticket from machine. Rush-hour fares $1-$1.05 on Blue or Yellow Line. Trains every 5-10 min. Allow 40 min total from airport to midtown destinations. Clean, quiet, comfortable coaches. Good choice if you're traveling light. **To Dulles Intl Airport** Washington Flyer hourly 5 am-10 pm. $12 OW, $20 RT. 35-50 min. **To BWI, Baltimore** Take Washington Flyer to Capitol Hilton Hotel (see above). Transfer to BWI bus. Service hourly from Capitol Hilton 5:30 am-11:30 pm. $12. 65 min to BWI.

🚗 Avis, Budget, Dollar, Hertz, National.

**P** ST $20, LT $6.

**To Fredericksburg** Groome Transportation, 800-552-7911 (Va). **To Virginia locations** Springfield, Ft. Belvoir, Quantico, FBI Academy, Stafford, Manassas: DAFRE Limo, 703-690-3102.

## WELLINGTON, New Zealand

Wellington Intl Airport, 4 mi (6 km) SE

🚖 NZ$15 ($9.95), 20 min. To Burma Lodge, NZ$20 ($13.25), 25-30 min.

🚌 Vickers Coach Lines every 20 min 6:30 am-9:50 pm M-F. NZ$4.20 ($2.80) paid before boarding. Sat 7:30 am-8 pm, Sun 7:30 am-10 pm, at 30-min intervals. Stops at any bus stop on request, RR station. Downtown, 10-15 min.

🚗 Avis, Budget, Hertz, Percy, Silver Fern, Town and Around, United.

P NZ$9 ($6)/day.


## WEST PALM BEACH, Florida

Palm Beach Intl Airport, 5 mi W of The Breakers

🚖 $7-8, 10-15 min.

🚗 Avis, Budget, Hertz, National.

P ST $8, LT $3.50.


## WHITE PLAINS, New York

Westchester County Airport, 4 mi NE

🚖 Downtown White Plains $14, 10-min ride. If no cab at airport call 592-8534 or 949-0110. Other fares: American Can, MCI $10; Armonk $14; Arrowwood $10; Chappaqua, Elmsford $19-25; Greenwich $17-23; JFK $55 plus tolls; LaGuardia $50 plus tolls; Pepsico $10; Rye Hilton $15; Stamford $22-30; Stouffer $14; Tarrytown $22.

🚐 Connecticut Limousine service to White Plains, New Rochelle, Rye, Tarrytown, Elmsford, Riverdale-Bronx. Info: 914-699-1000.

🚆 **To New York City** Metro North Commuter train to Grand Central Terminal $5 peak, $3.75 off-peak. Frequencies from 10 min rush hours to 60 min late night, weekends. Operates 5 am-midnight.

🚗 Avis, Budget, Dollar, Hertz, National, Snappy.

**P** $4/day.

## WICHITA, Kansas
Wichita Mid-Continent Airport, 6 mi SW

🚖 $7.50, addl passengers $1 each. 10-15 min.

🚗 Avis, Budget, Dollar, Enterprise, Hertz, National, Thrifty.

## WILLEMSTAD, Curacao
Curacao Intl Airport, 4.5 mi (7 km) NW

🚖 Naf18 ($10), 18 min; to Princess Beach Hotel, Naf19 ($10.50), 25 min; to Caribbean Hotel, Naf16 ($9), 15 min. Taxis have TX on plate and Taxi sign on roof. One fare covers 4 passengers; 5 adds 25% to fare, 6 adds 50% to fare. 25% surcharge 11 pm-6 am. Baggage: if unable to close trunk, $1 each extra bag.

🚌 ABC Co. bus departs hourly 6 am-11 pm next to arrivals hall. Pay driver Naf70 (40¢). Baggage OK. To Otrabanda, 20 min; to Punda, 1 hr.

🚗 Avis, Budget, Caribe, Hertz, National, Ric-Car, Ruiz, Uralco.

**P** Naf8 ($4.50)/day.

# WILMINGTON, Delaware
Greater Wilmington Airport, 5 mi S

🚗 $14, 10-12 min. If no cab at airport, use courtesy phone.

🚕 Avis, Budget, Dollar, Snappy.


# WINNIPEG, Manitoba
Winnipeg Intl Airport, 4 mi W

🚗 C$7 ($5.25), 15 min.

🚐 Kidd Limousine Service, C$7 ($5.25) to downtown hotels.

🚌 No. 15 Sargent bus about every 25 min. C$1.50 ($1.20). 17-min ride downtown.

🚕 Avis, Hertz, Mutual, Tasman.


# YOUNGSTOWN, Ohio
Youngstown Municipal Airport, 14 mi N

🚗 $18 flat fare, 30 min to downtown Youngstown.

🚕 Avis, Budget, Hertz, National, Snappy.


# ZAGREB, Yugoslavia
Zagreb Airport, 10.6 mi (17 km) SE

🚗 Din67300 ($12), 25 min.

🚐 JAT bus every 30 min, 7 am to last flight. 25 min to JAT air terminal, Central Bus Terminal. Hotel Zagreb Intercontinental operates courtesy transport to and from airport.

🚌 No. 267 to ZET terminal (main RR) every 1-2 hrs early morning, afternoon-evening. 50¢.

🚗 Autotehna-Avis, Autotourist, Inex, InterRent, Kompas-Hertz, Putnik, Unis.

## ZURICH, Switzerland
Zurich Airport (Kloten), 7.5 mi (12 km) N

🚕 SF29 ($19), 15-20 min depending on traffic. If fare includes tip, a sign near meter will say so. Otherwise tip 10%.

🚆 Look for railway sign outside customs—station is beneath airport. Train every 10-20 min 6:06 am-midnight. 10 minutes into Zurich. Excellent service. Fares SF4.30 ($2.85) 2nd class, SF6.50 ($4.30) 1st class. Little difference in comfort though 2nd class may be more crowded. **Direct rail services** From airport station to many destinations in Switzerland including Lucerne, Lausanne, Geneva, Bern, Interlaken, Chur. Baggage-Fly rail luggage service to and from 100+ rail stations all over Switzerland operates at Zurich and Geneva Flughafen stations.

🚌 No. 68 bus to city every 9 min rush hours, 15-30 min other times. SF2.50 ($1.65).

🚗 Avis, Budget, Europcar, Hertz, InterRent.

P ST SF11 ($7.25), LT SF8 ($5.25).